SPARTANS

Written By Don McLeese
Illustrated By Chris Marrinan

ROURKE PUBLISHING

Vero Beach, Florida 32964

www.rourkepublishing.com

Edited by Katherine M. Thal
Illustrated by Chris Marrinan
Art Direction and Page Layout by Renee Brady

Photo Credits: © Marie-france Bélanger: 4, 5, 26, 27, 28, 29, 30, 31, 32; © paradoks_blizanaca: 26; © Dianna Toney: 27; © Pavlos Rekas: 28

Library of Congress Cataloging-in-Publication Data

McLeese, Don.
  Spartans / Don McLeese.
    p. cm. -- (Warriors graphic illustrated)
  Includes bibliographical references and index.
  ISBN 978-1-60694-436-3 (alk. paper)
  ISBN 978-1-60694-545-2 (soft cover)
  1. Sparta (Extinct city)--History, Military--Juvenile literature. 2. Soldiers--Greece--Sparta (Extinct city)--Juvenile literature. 3. Greece--History, Military--To 146 B.C.--Juvenile literature. 4. Graphic novels. I. Title.
  DF261.S8M38 2010
  938'.9--dc22
                                      2009020498

Printed in the USA

CG/CG

www.rourkepublishing.com - rourke@rourkepublishing.com
Post Office Box 643328 Vero Beach, Florida 32964

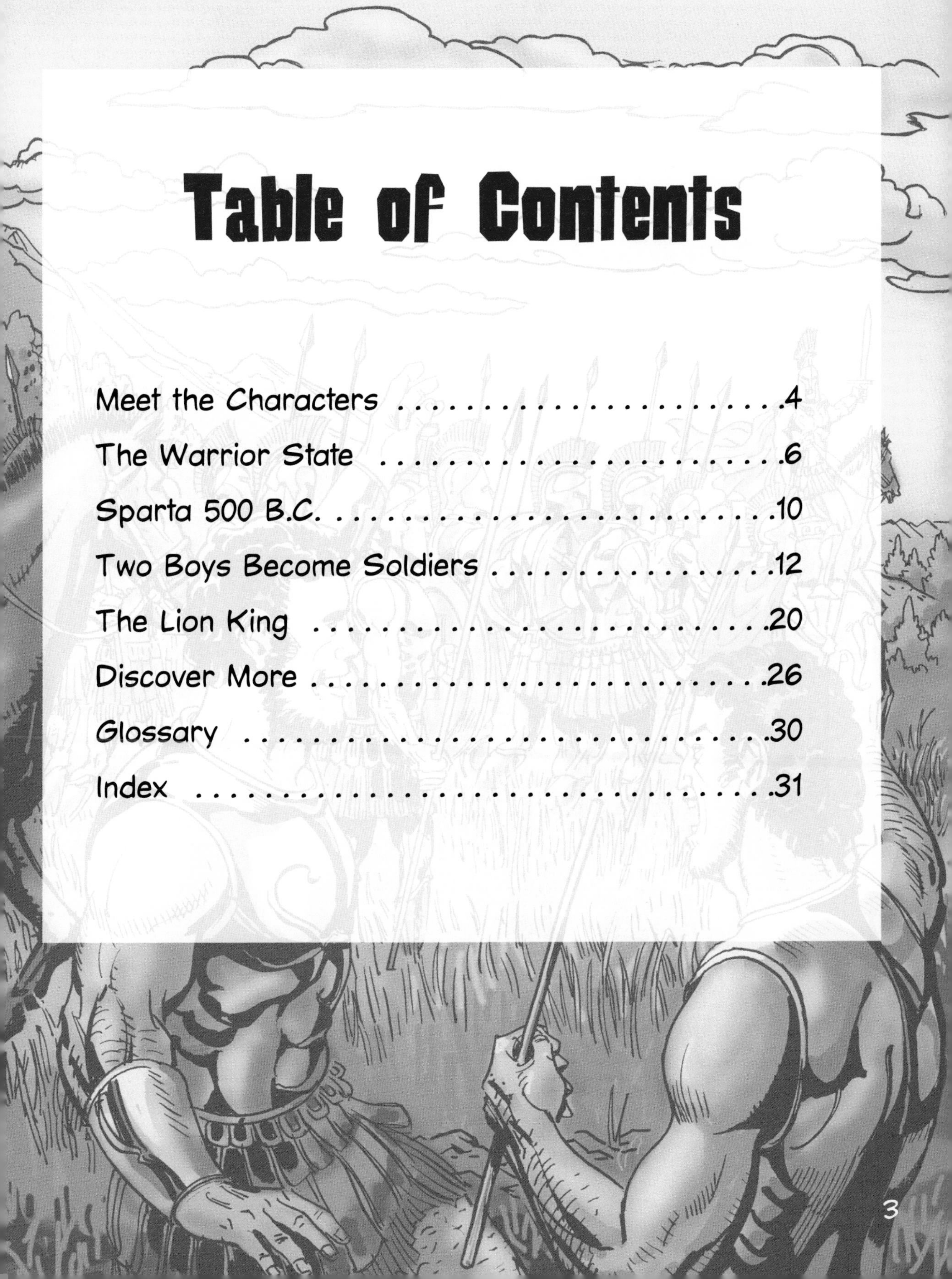

Table of Contents

Meet the Characters 4

The Warrior State 6

Sparta 500 B.C. 10

Two Boys Become Soldiers 12

The Lion King 20

Discover More 26

Glossary 30

Index 31

MEET THE CHARACTERS

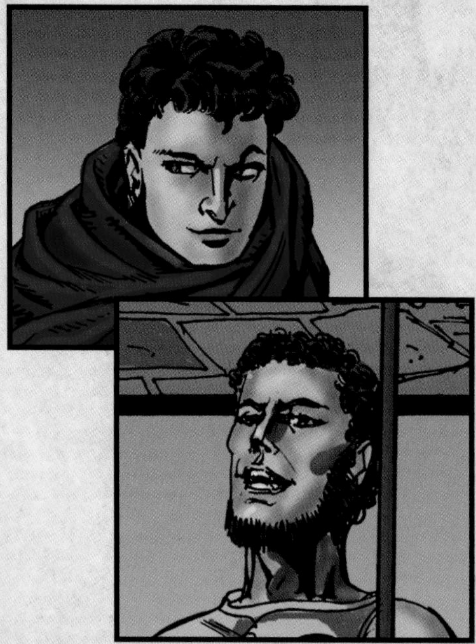

Aristotle

Aristotle is a little older than Plato and is the strong, tough leader of his military pack.

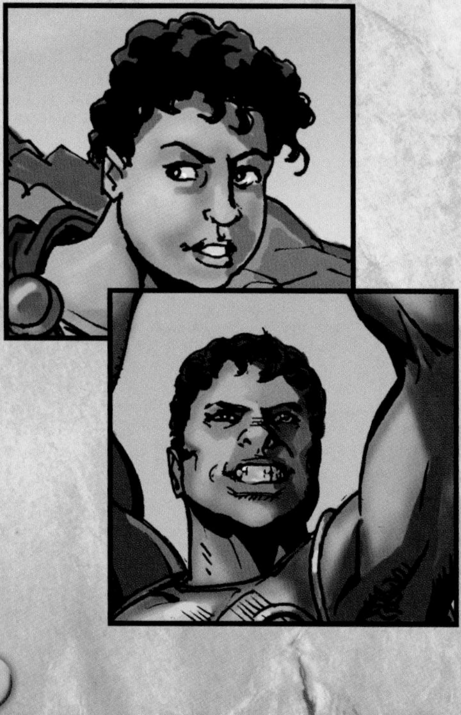

Plato

Plato, a sweet boy, is just seven and has to learn how to survive on his own in the military.

Note: Aristotle and Plato are well known Greek names. These characters are fictional in this book and are not the famous philosophers named Aristotle and Plato.

Spartan Mother

Plato's mother is a typical Spartan mother who worries over sending her young son to the military. She is a fictional character.

King Leonidas

King Leonidas was the King of Sparta. He is famous for his stand against the Persian Army in 480 B.C. While this story is historical fiction, King Leonidas was a real person. You can find out more about him by reading history books.

THE WARRIOR STATE

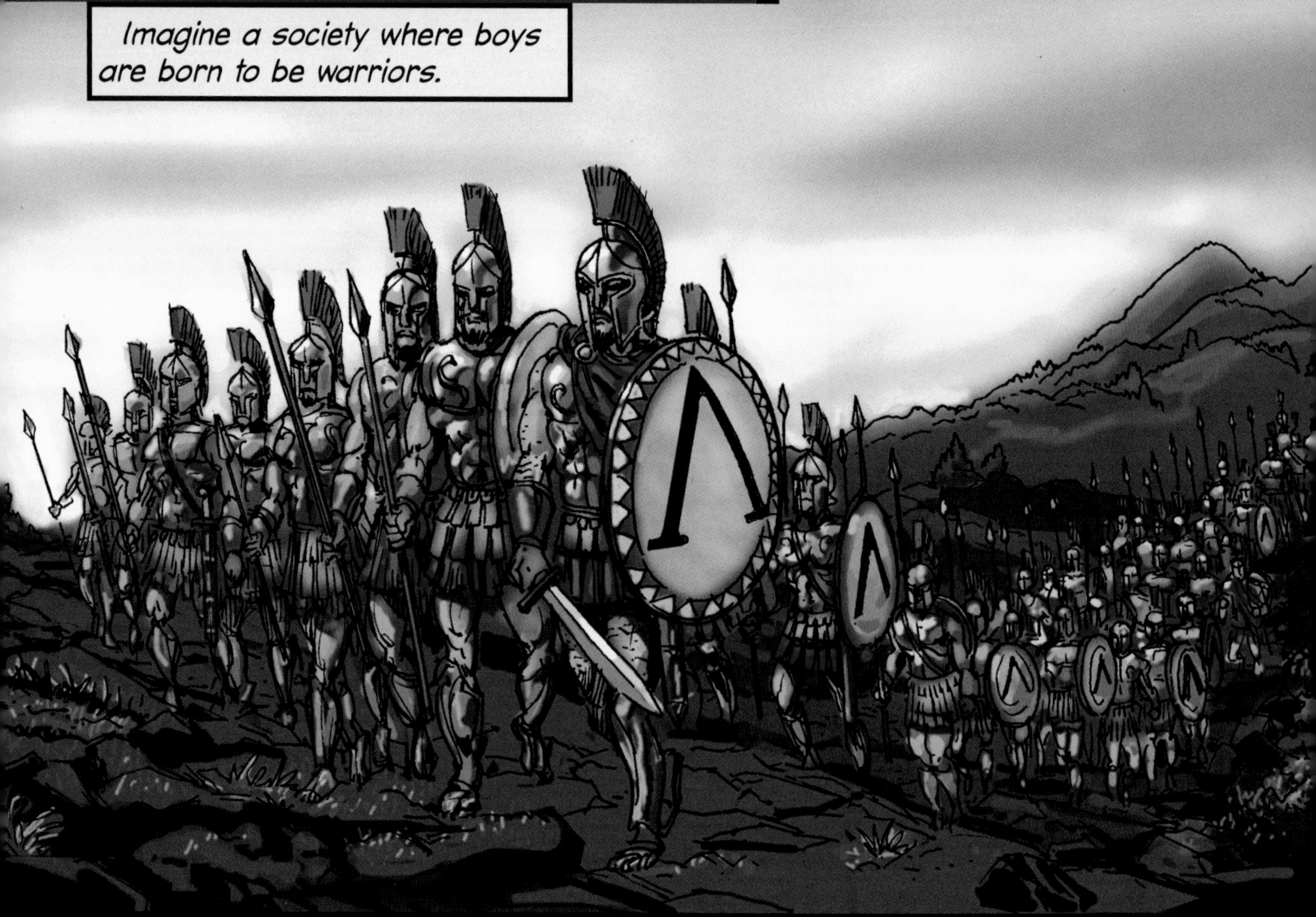
Imagine a society where boys are born to be warriors.

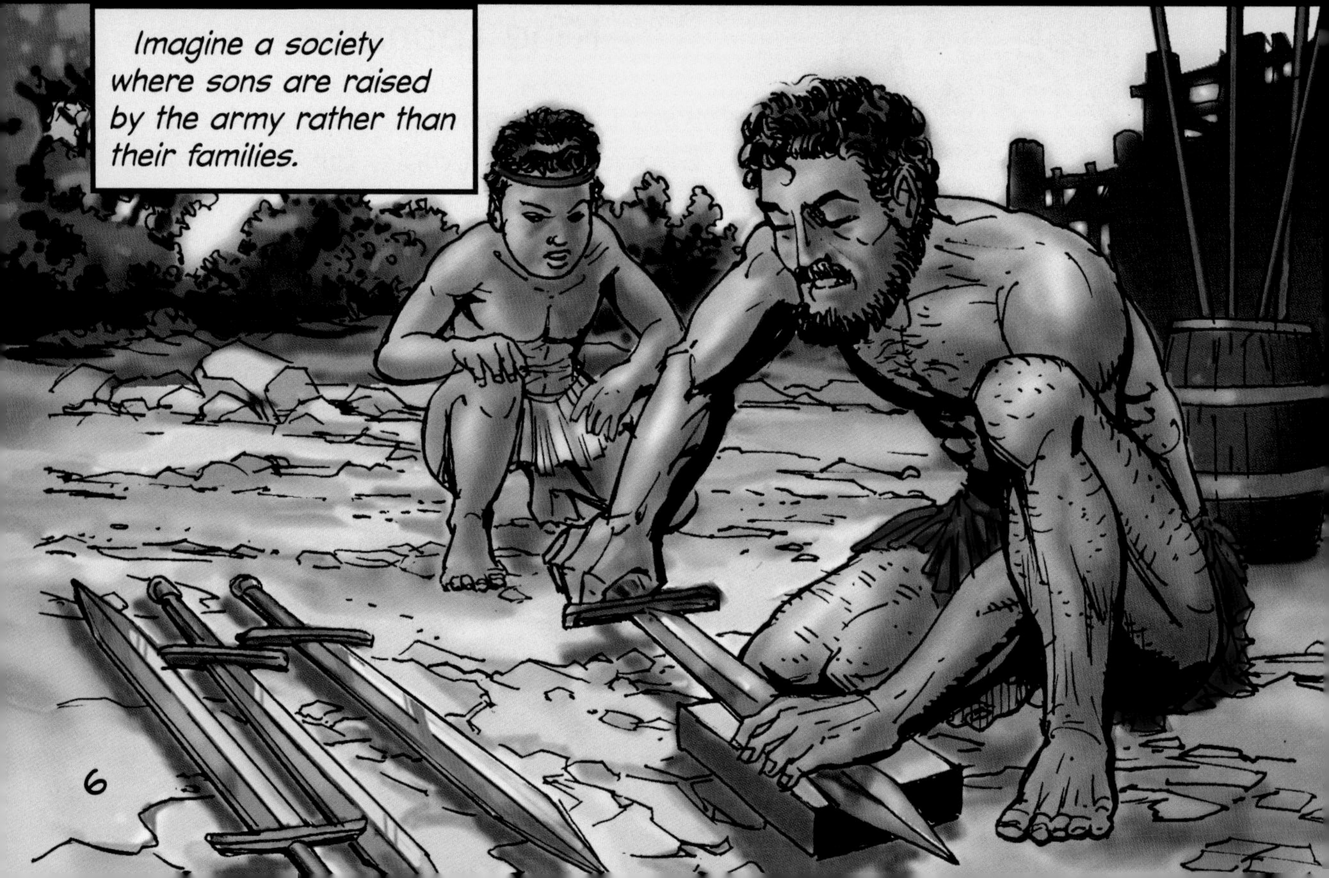
Imagine a society where sons are raised by the army rather than their families.

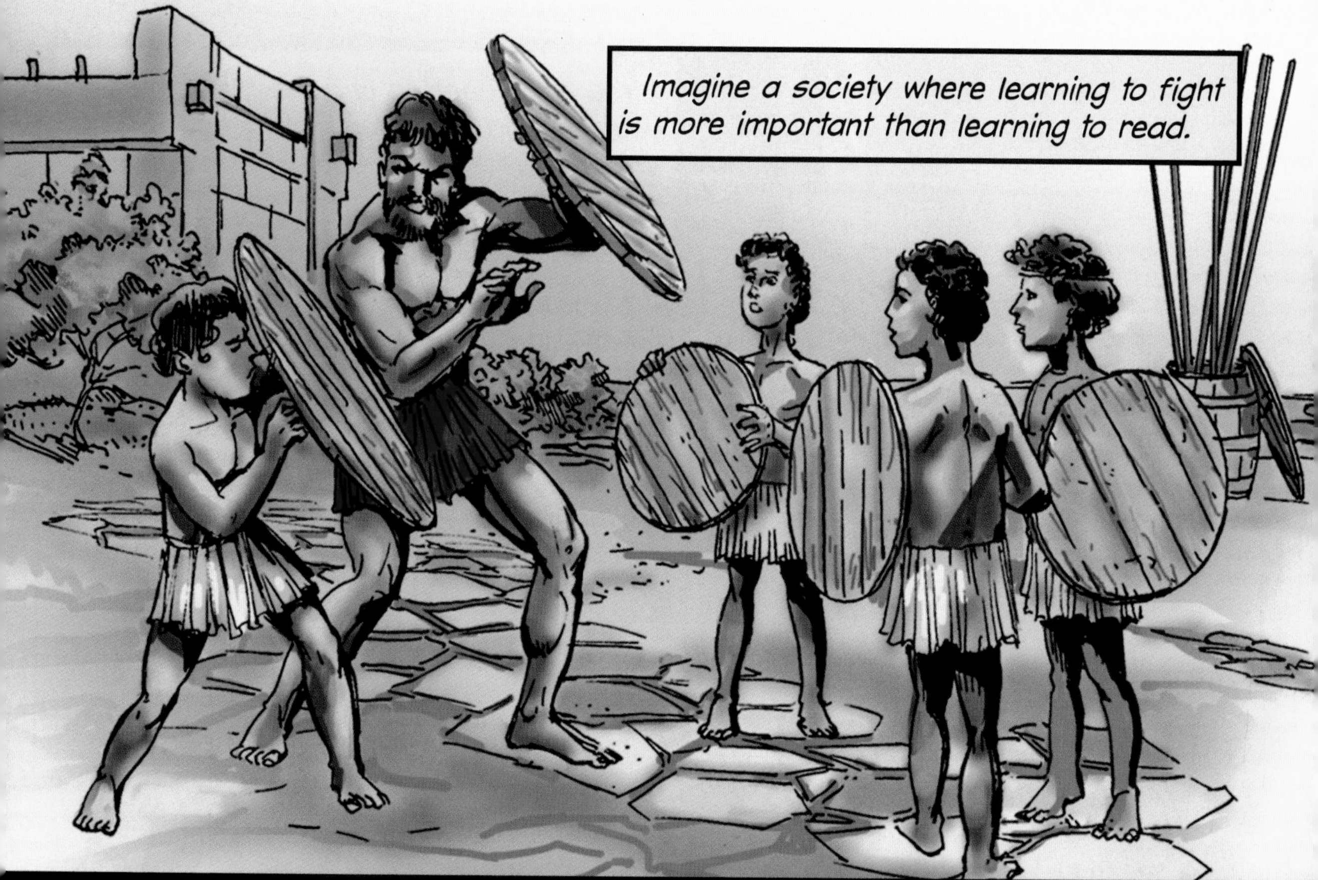
Imagine a society where learning to fight is more important than learning to read.

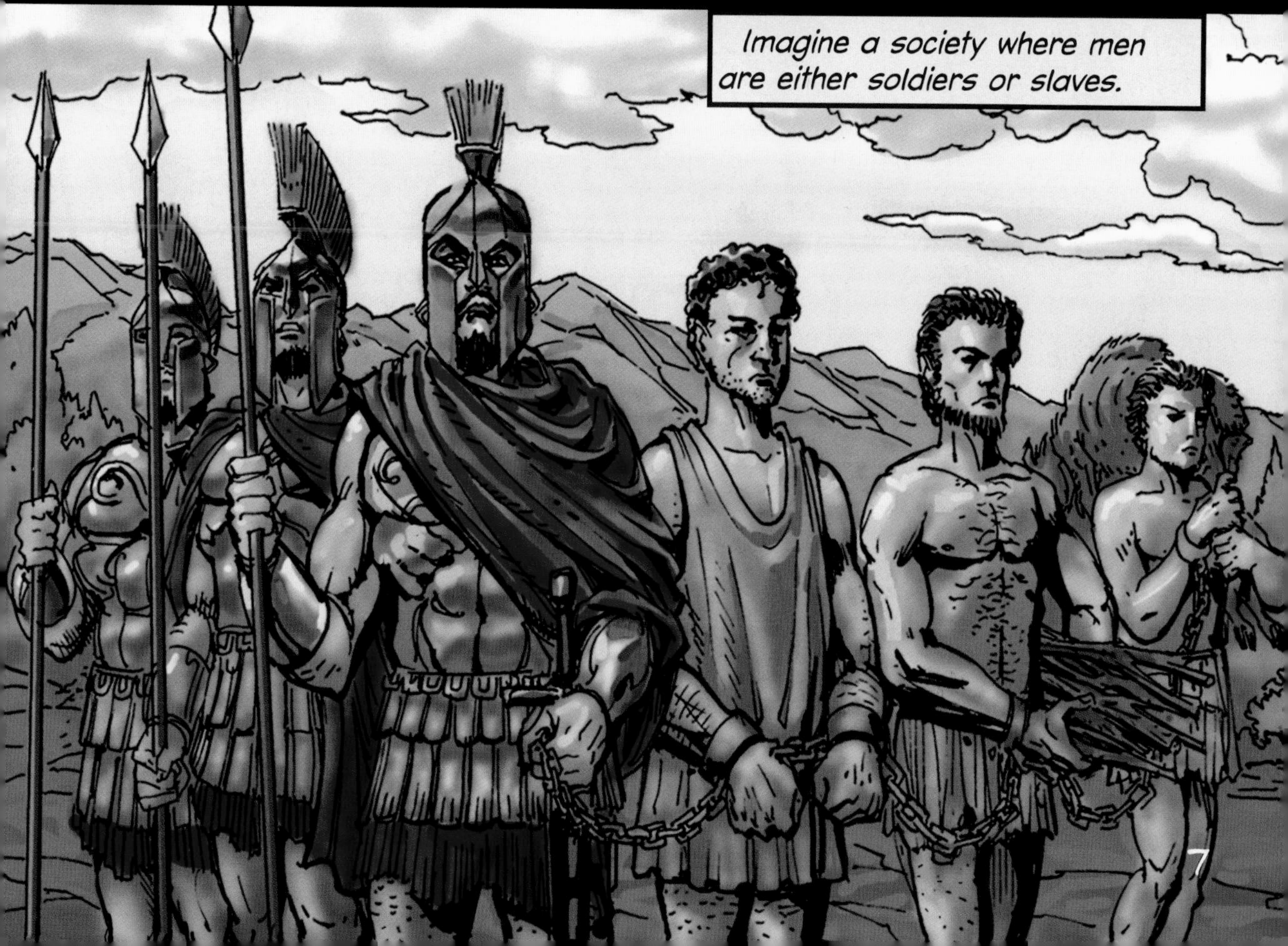
Imagine a society where men are either soldiers or slaves.

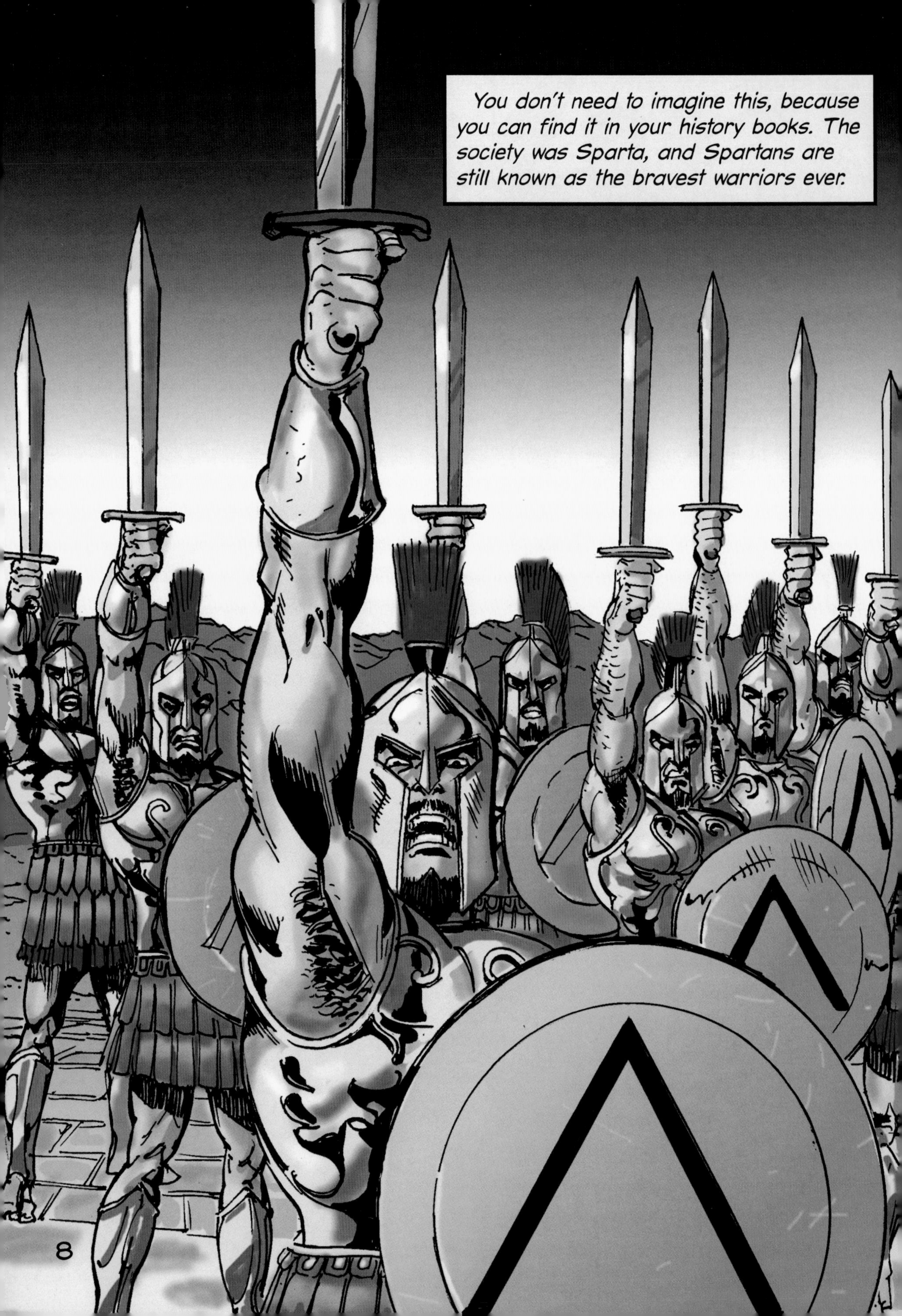
You don't need to imagine this, because you can find it in your history books. The society was Sparta, and Spartans are still known as the bravest warriors ever.

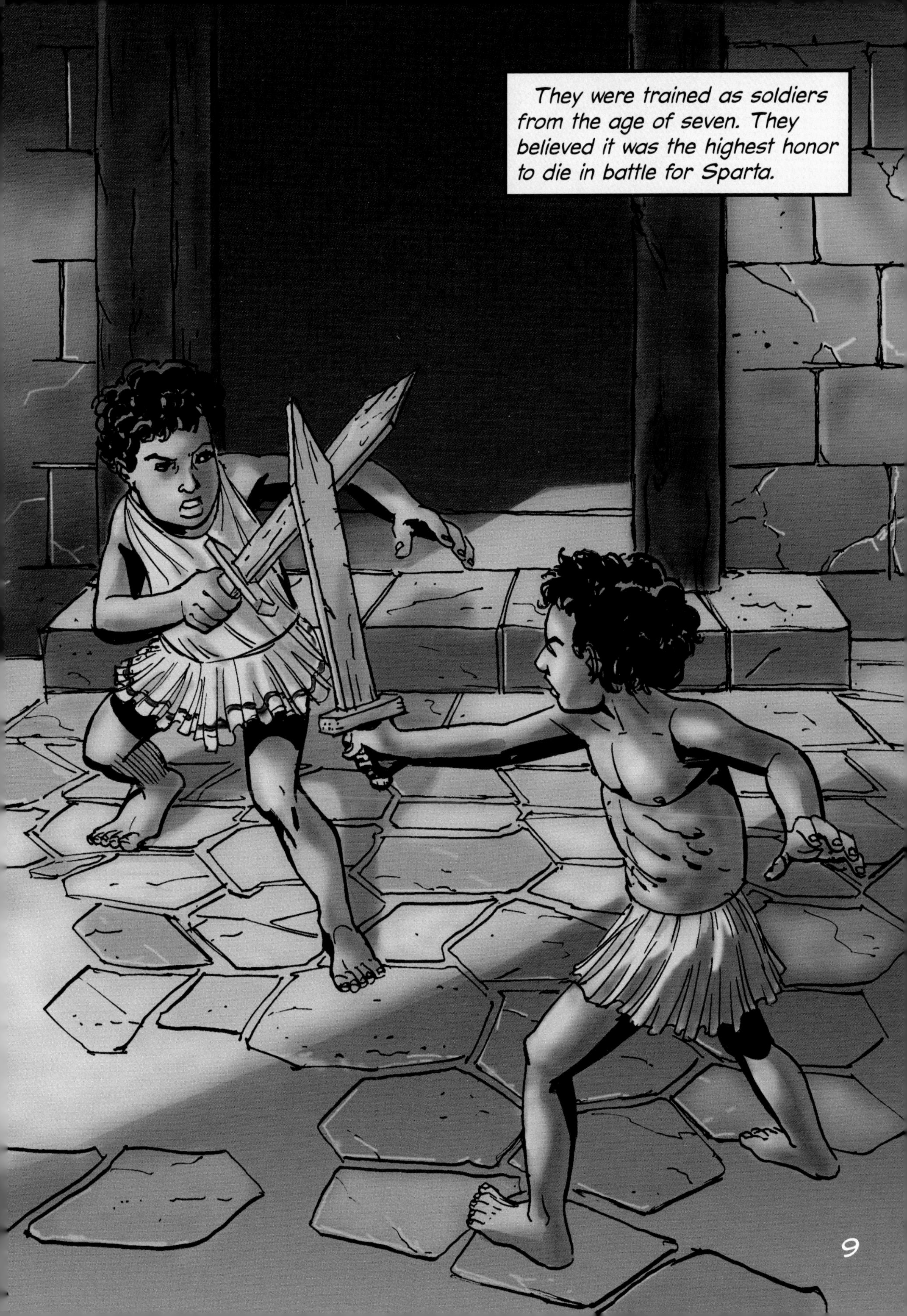
They were trained as soldiers from the age of seven. They believed it was the highest honor to die in battle for Sparta.

SPARTA 500 B.C.

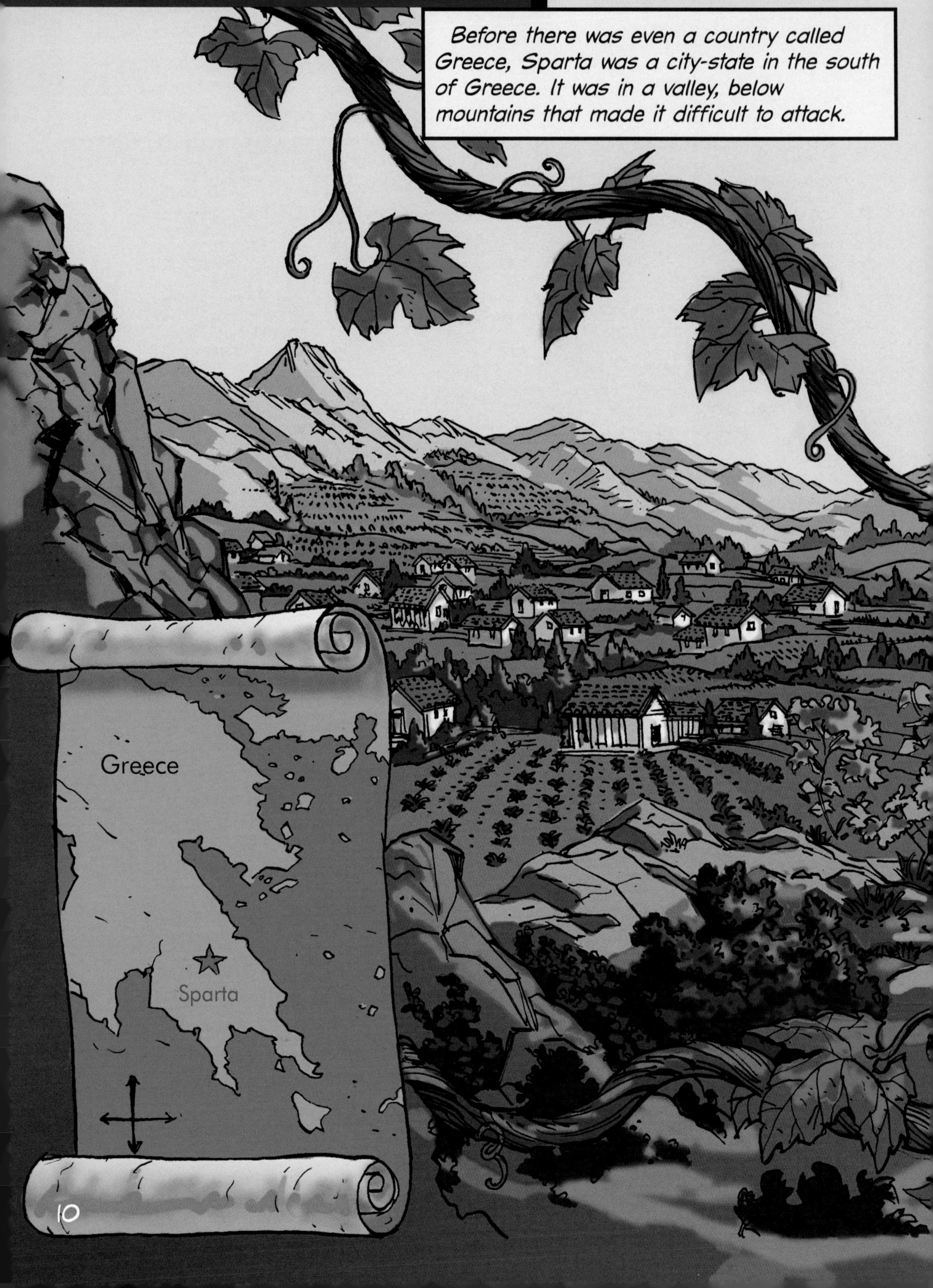
Before there was even a country called Greece, Sparta was a city-state in the south of Greece. It was in a valley, below mountains that made it difficult to attack.
Greece
Sparta

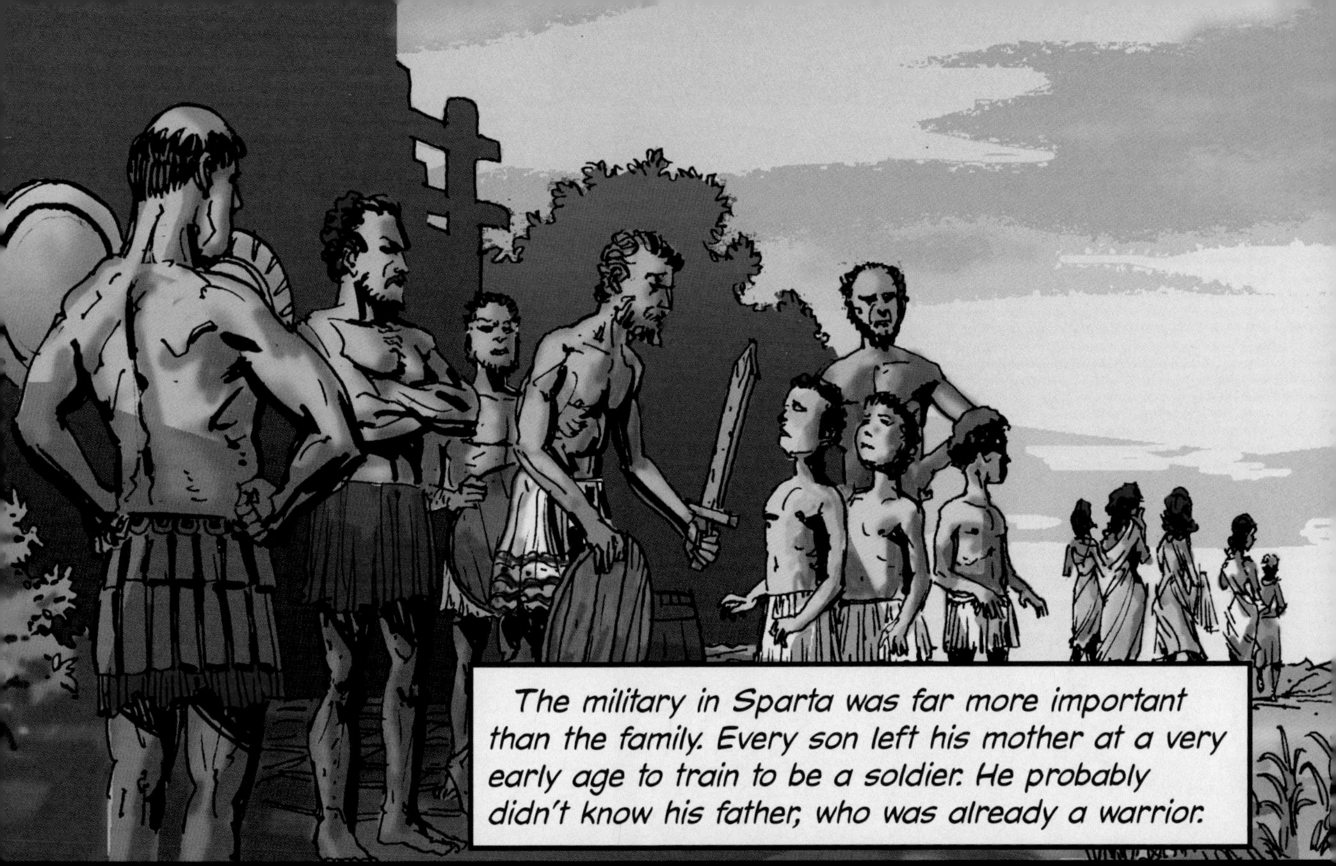
The military in Sparta was far more important than the family. Every son left his mother at a very early age to train to be a soldier. He probably didn't know his father, who was already a warrior.

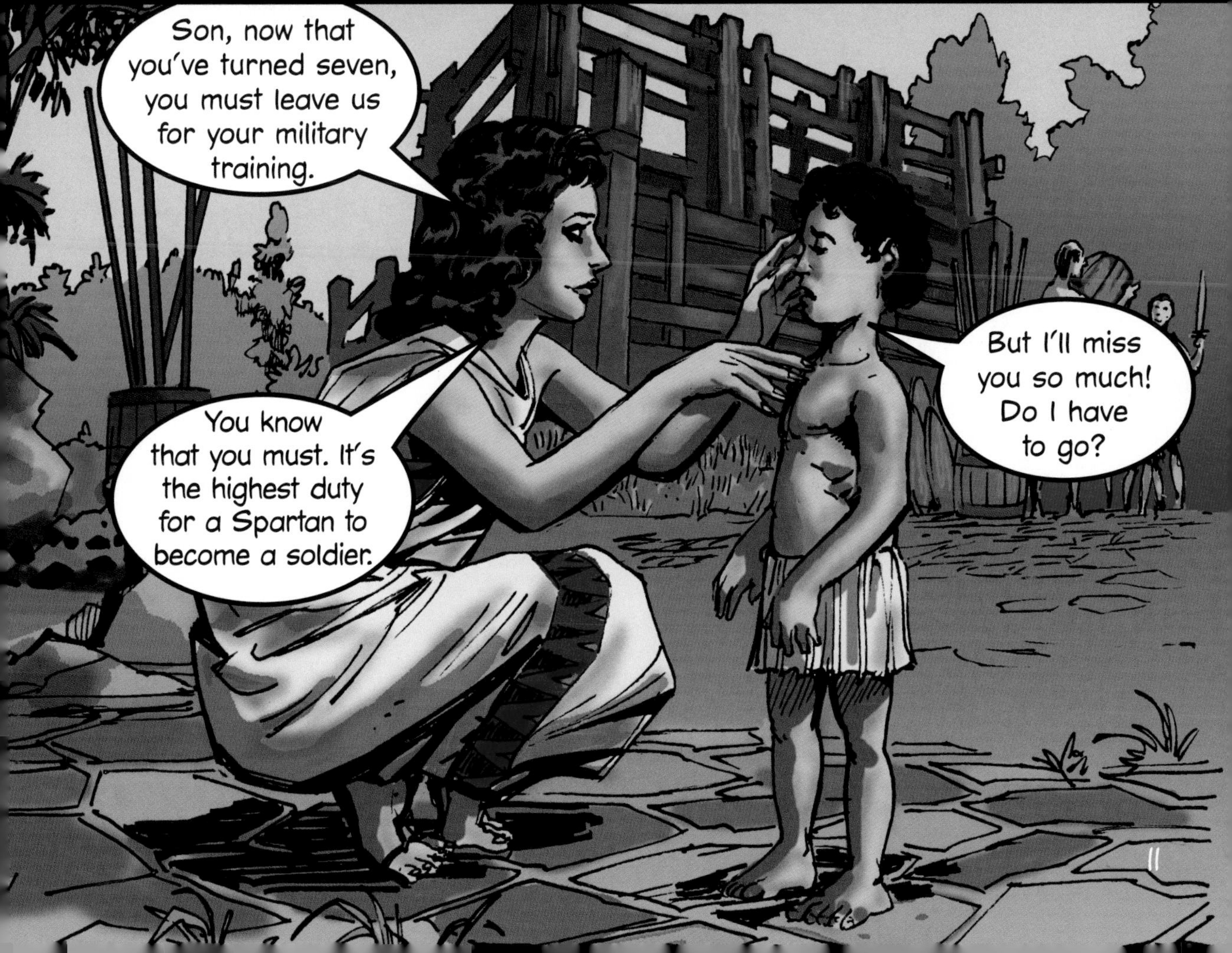
Son, now that you've turned seven, you must leave us for your military training.
You know that you must. It's the highest duty for a Spartan to become a soldier.
But I'll miss you so much! Do I have to go?

TWO BOYS BECOME SOLDIERS

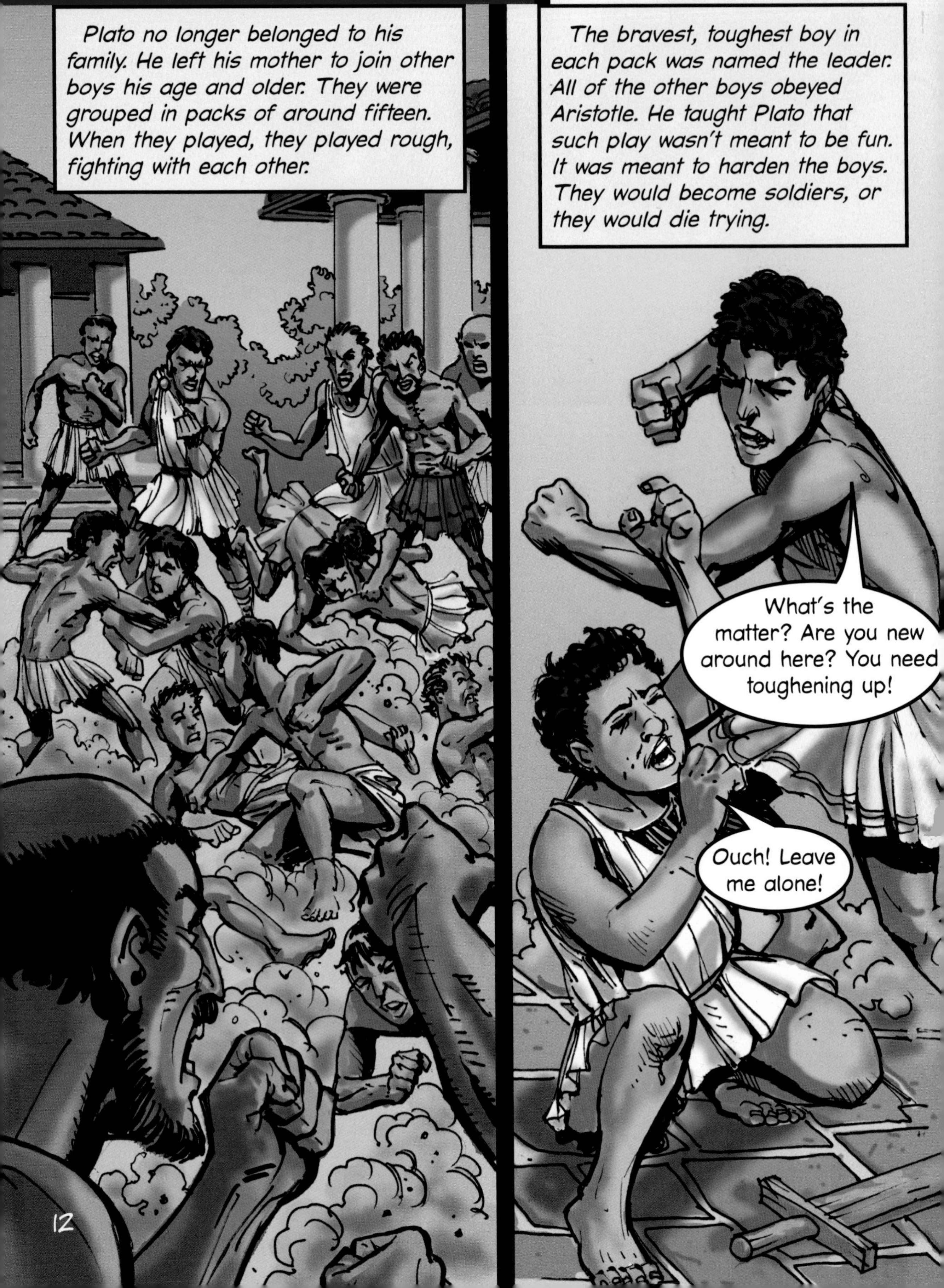

Plato no longer belonged to his family. He left his mother to join other boys his age and older. They were grouped in packs of around fifteen. When they played, they played rough, fighting with each other.
The bravest, toughest boy in each pack was named the leader. All of the other boys obeyed Aristotle. He taught Plato that such play wasn't meant to be fun. It was meant to harden the boys. They would become soldiers, or they would die trying.
What's the matter? Are you new around here? You need toughening up!
Ouch! Leave me alone!

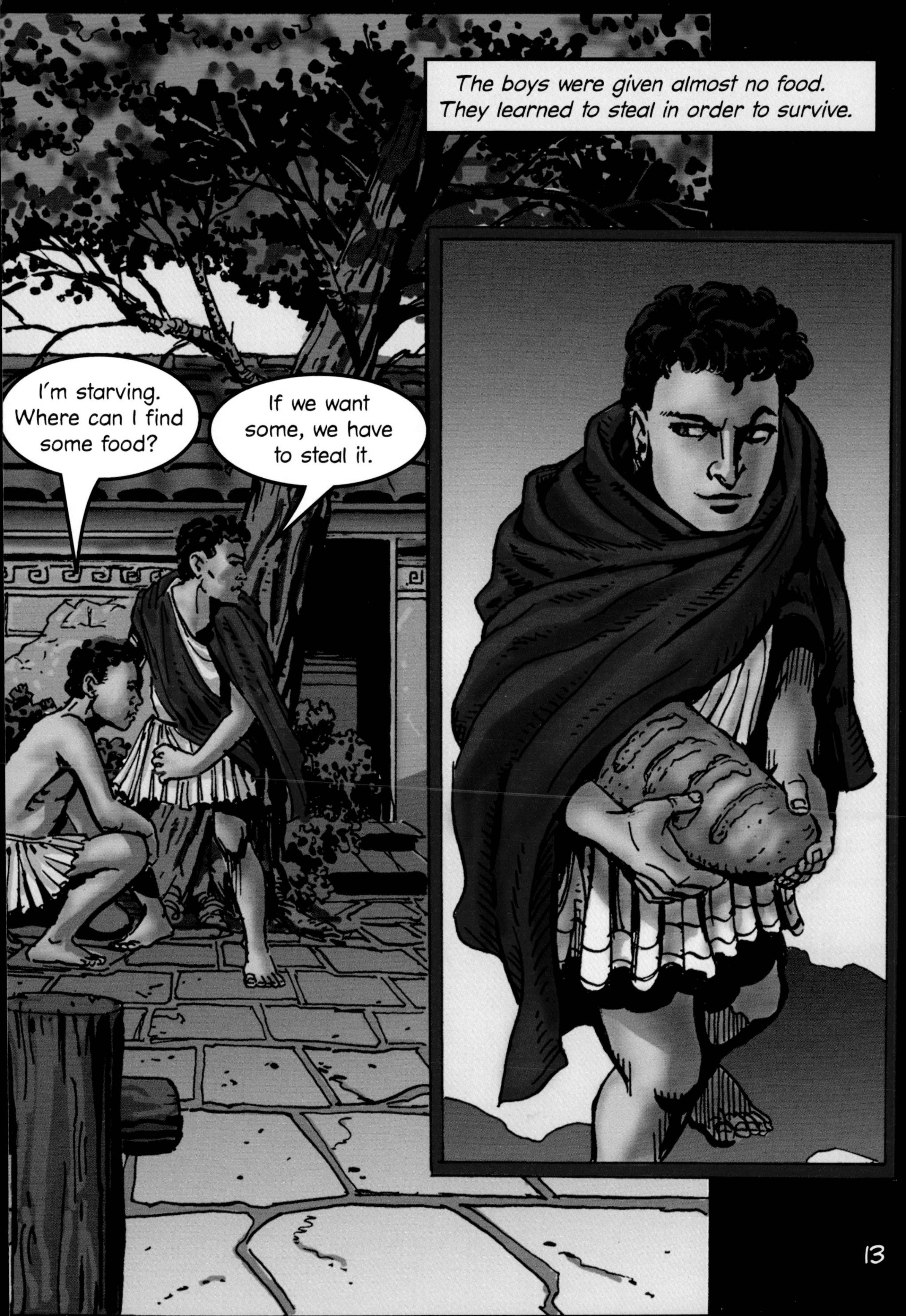

The boys were given almost no food. They learned to steal in order to survive.
I'm starving. Where can I find some food?
If we want some, we have to steal it.

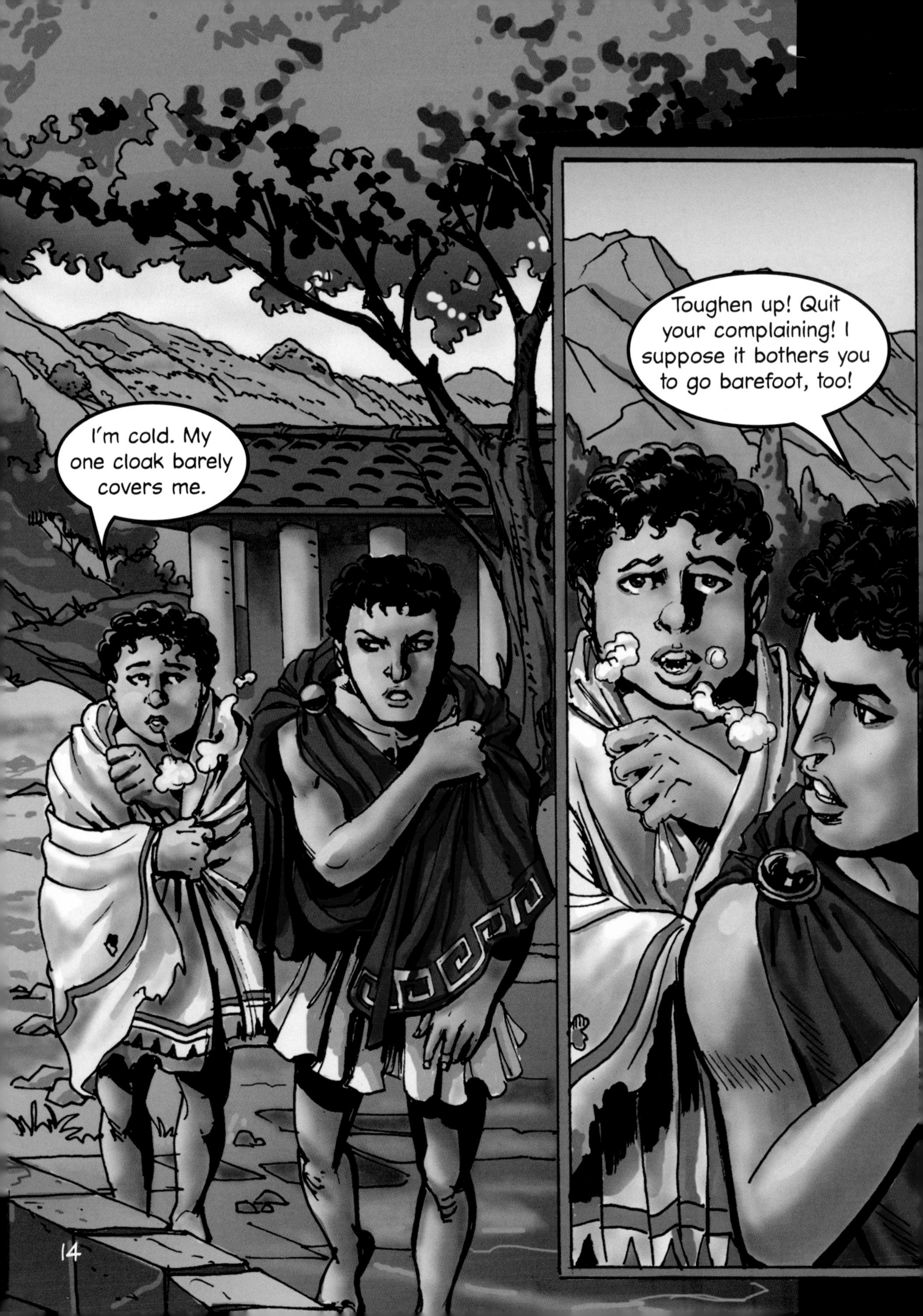
I'm cold. My one cloak barely covers me.
Toughen up! Quit your complaining! I suppose it bothers you to go barefoot, too!

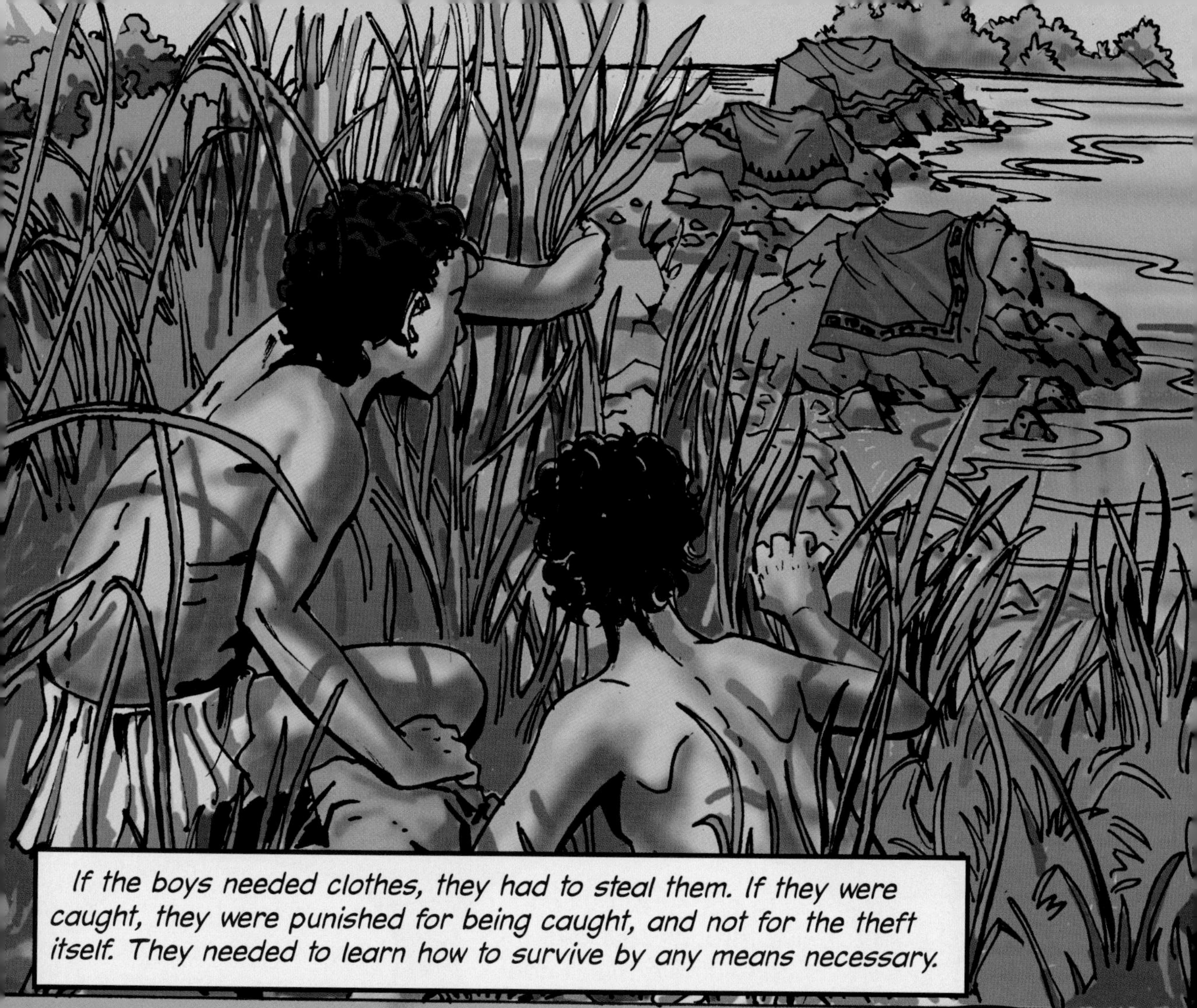
If the boys needed clothes, they had to steal them. If they were caught, they were punished for being caught, and not for the theft itself. They needed to learn how to survive by any means necessary.

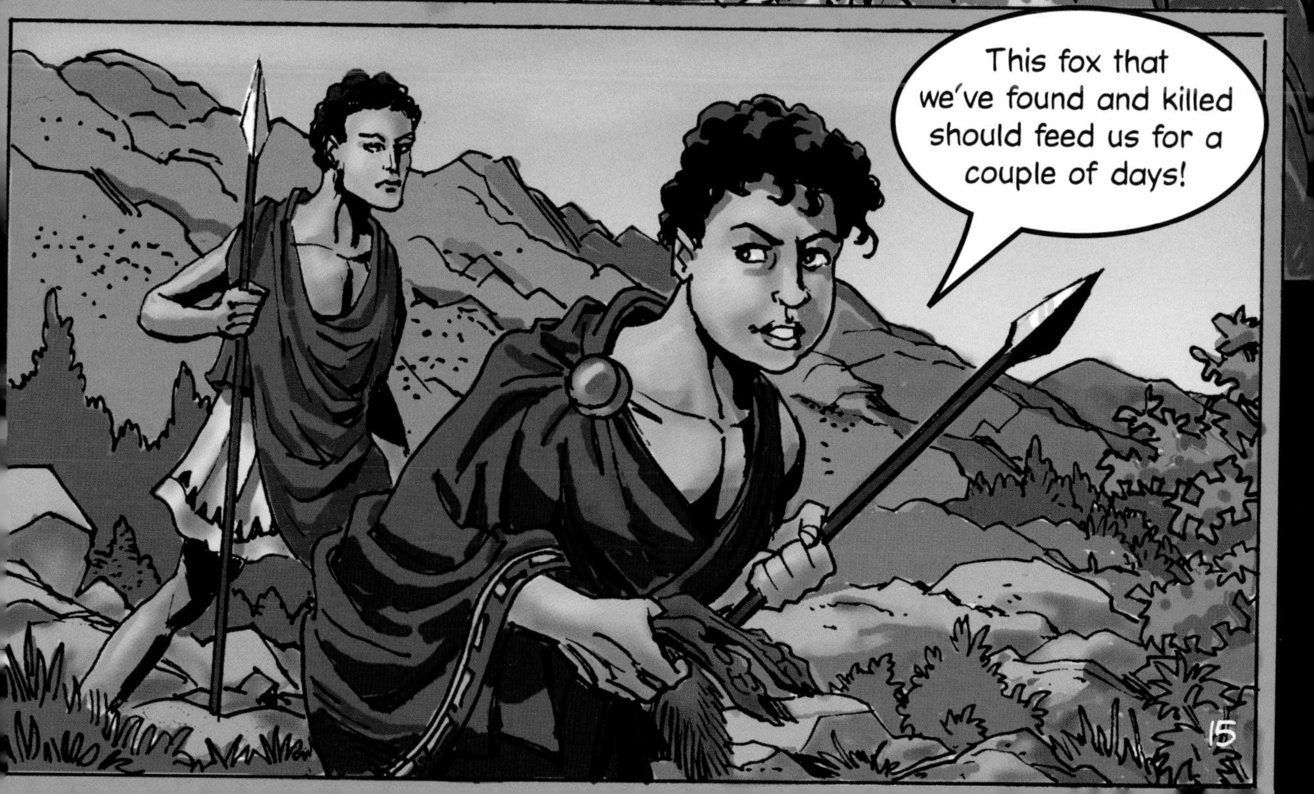
This fox that we've found and killed should feed us for a couple of days!

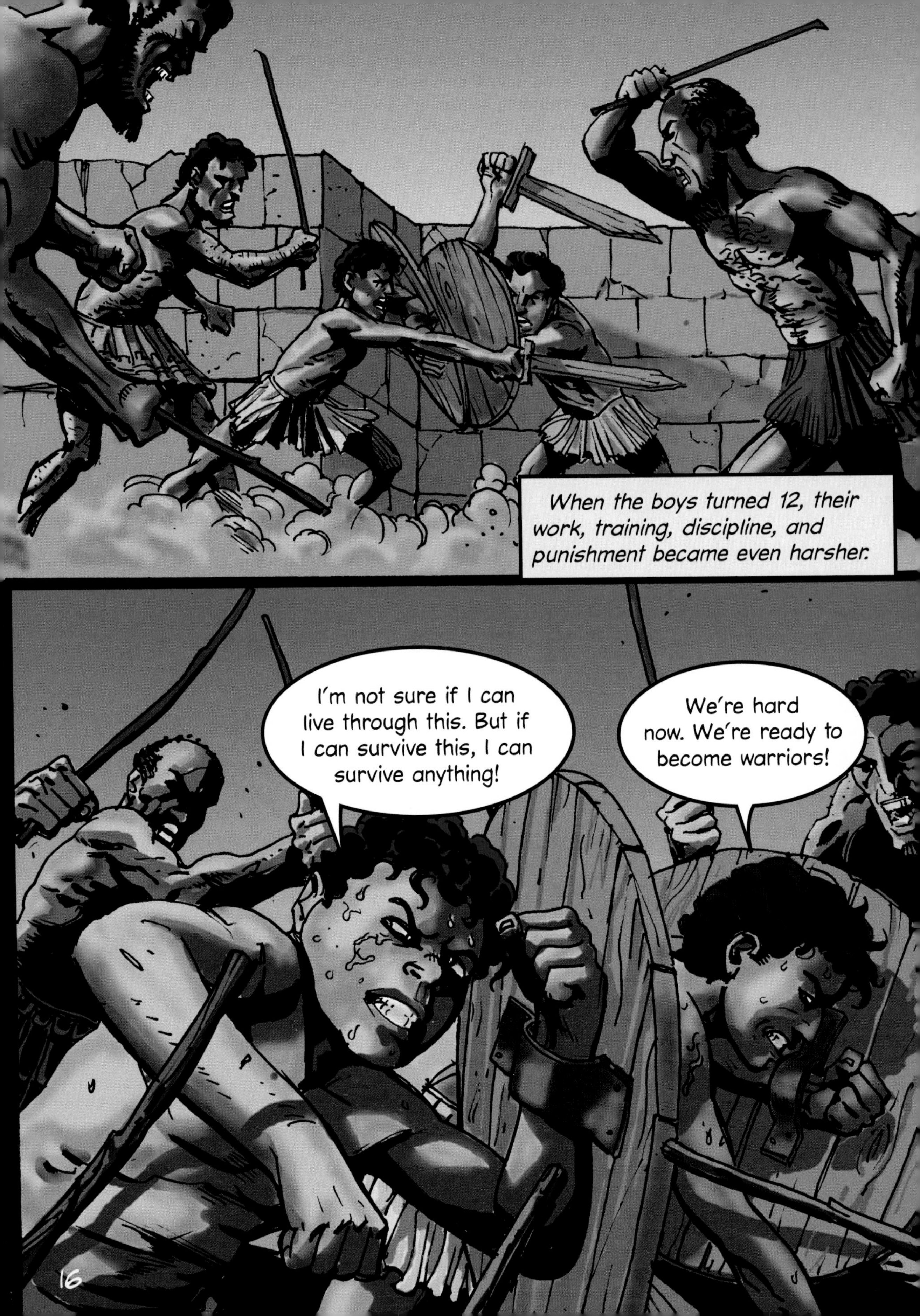
When the boys turned 12, their work, training, discipline, and punishment became even harsher.
I'm not sure if I can live through this. But if I can survive this, I can survive anything!
We're hard now. We're ready to become warriors!

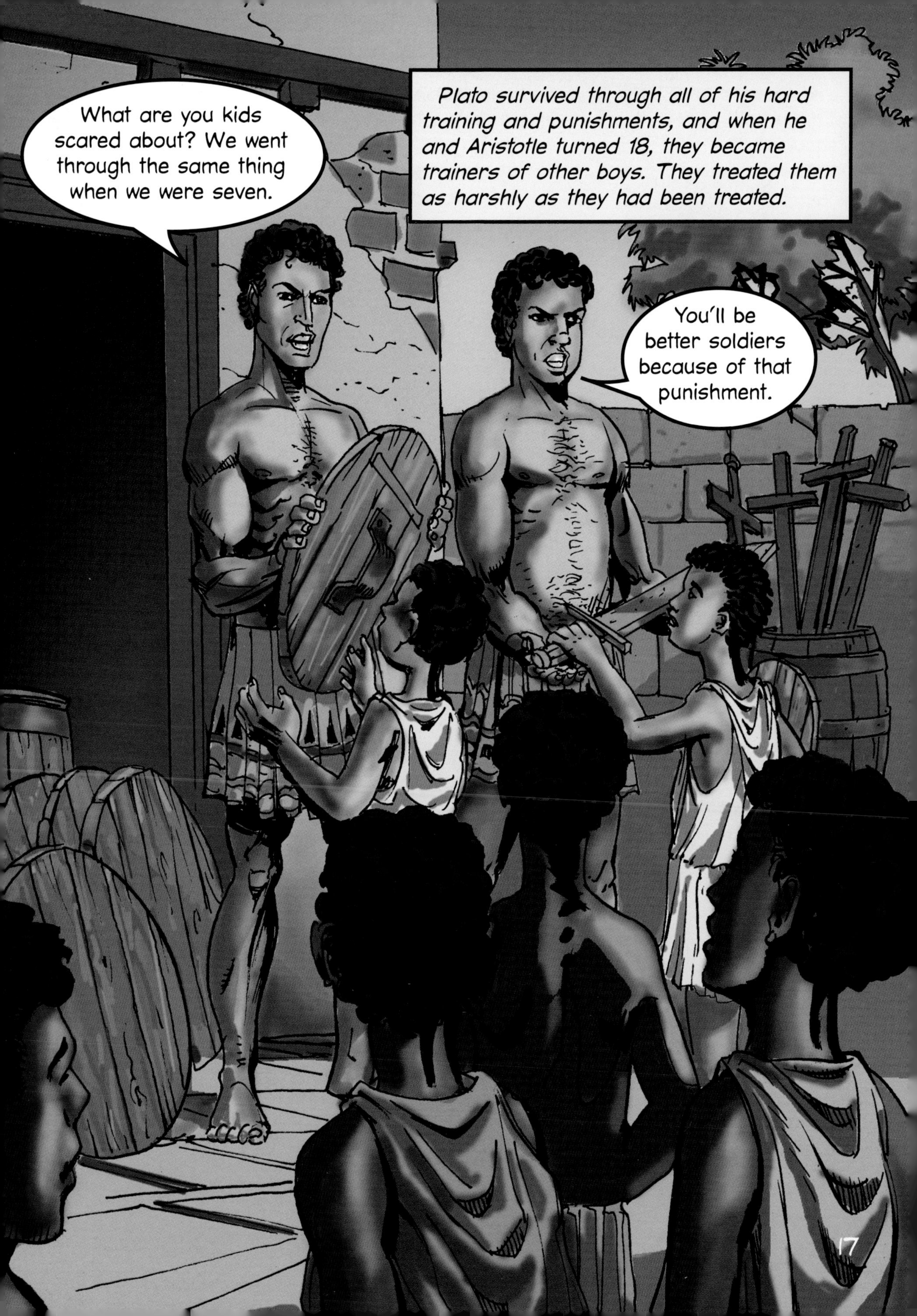
Plato survived through all of his hard training and punishments, and when he and Aristotle turned 18, they became trainers of other boys. They treated them as harshly as they had been treated.
What are you kids scared about? We went through the same thing when we were seven.
You'll be better soldiers because of that punishment.

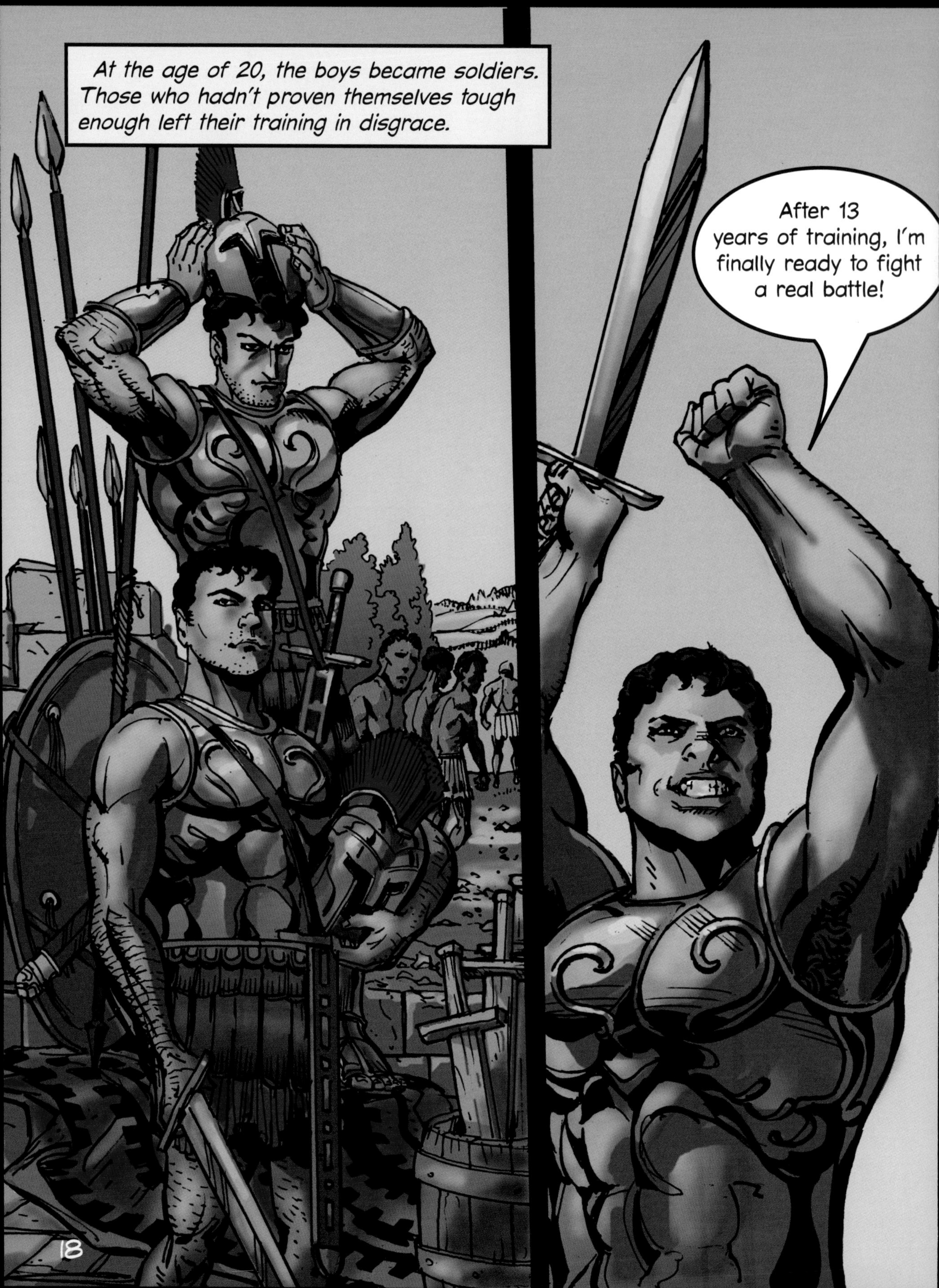
At the age of 20, the boys became soldiers. Those who hadn't proven themselves tough enough left their training in disgrace.
After 13 years of training, I'm finally ready to fight a real battle!

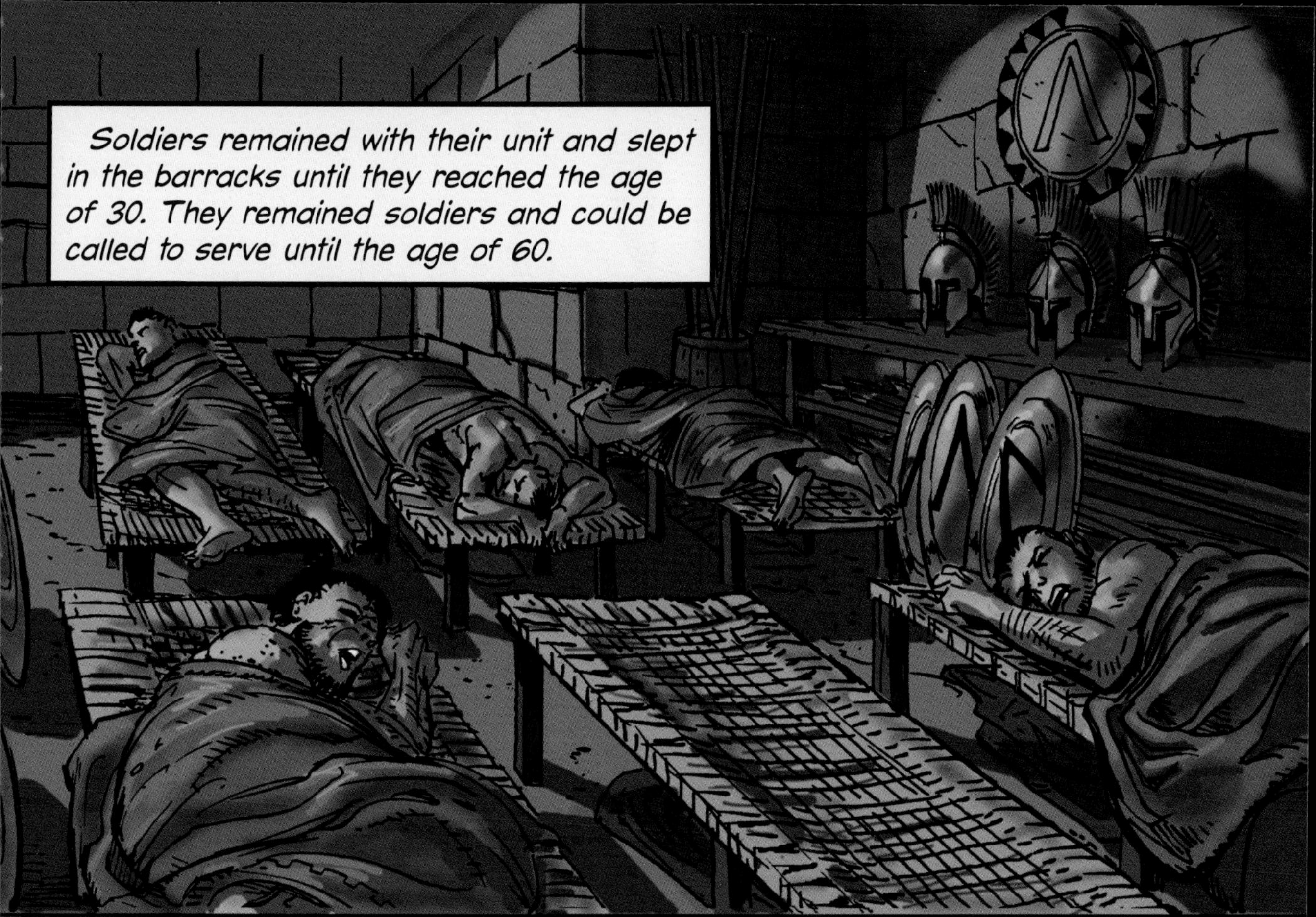
Soldiers remained with their unit and slept in the barracks until they reached the age of 30. They remained soldiers and could be called to serve until the age of 60.

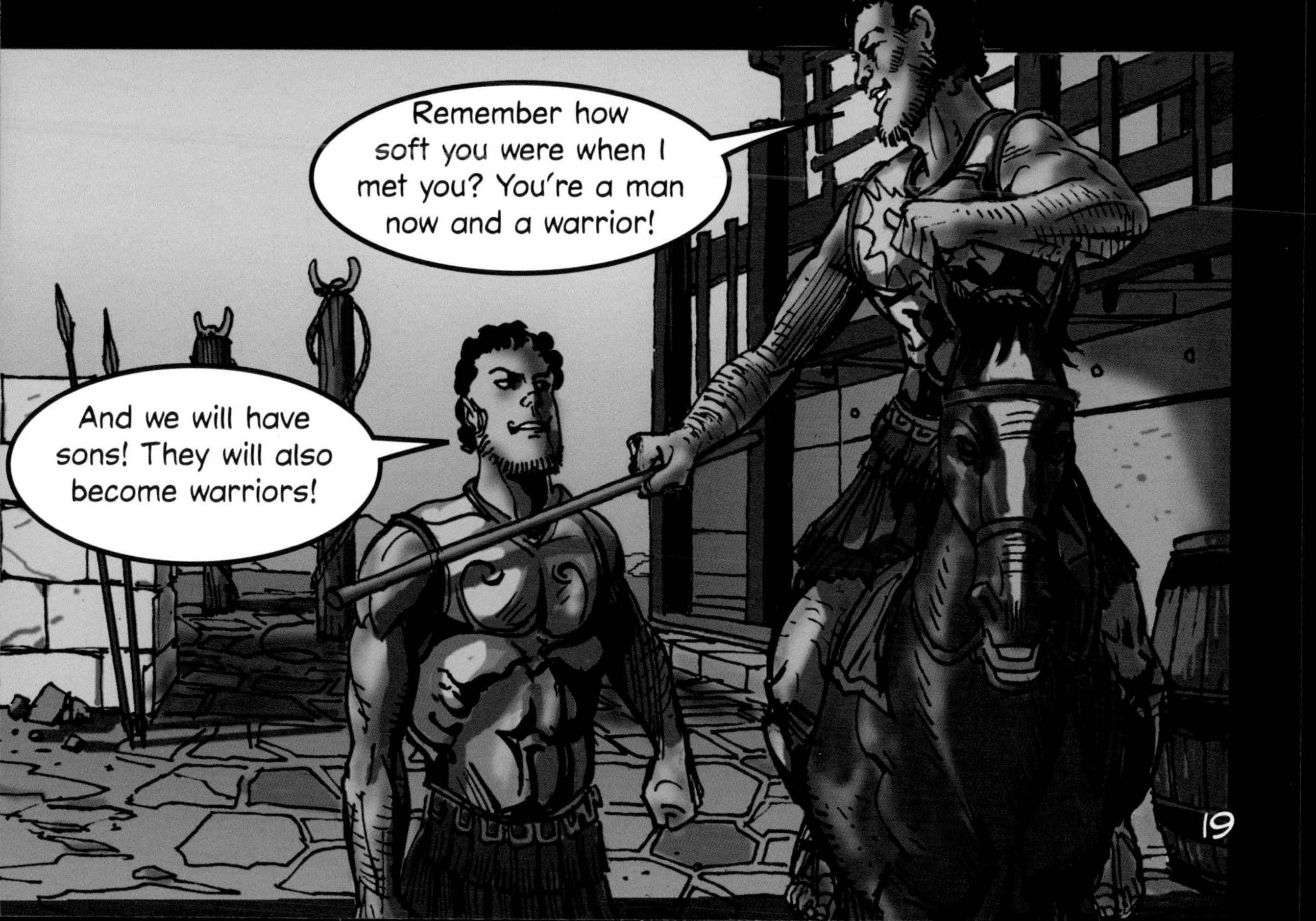
Remember how soft you were when I met you? You're a man now and a warrior!
And we will have sons! They will also become warriors!

THE LION KING

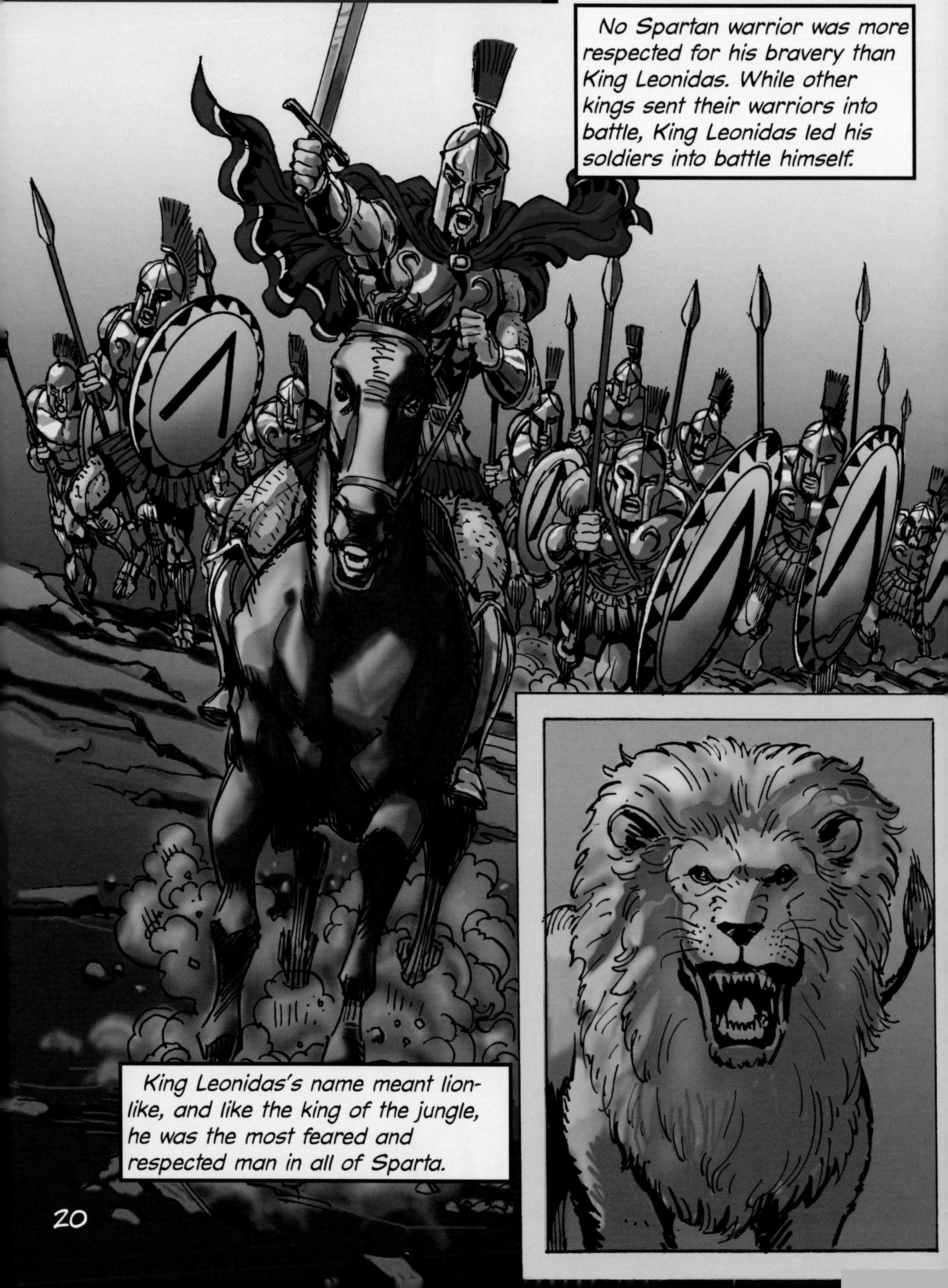
No Spartan warrior was more respected for his bravery than King Leonidas. While other kings sent their warriors into battle, King Leonidas led his soldiers into battle himself.
King Leonidas's name meant lion-like, and like the king of the jungle, he was the most feared and respected man in all of Sparta.

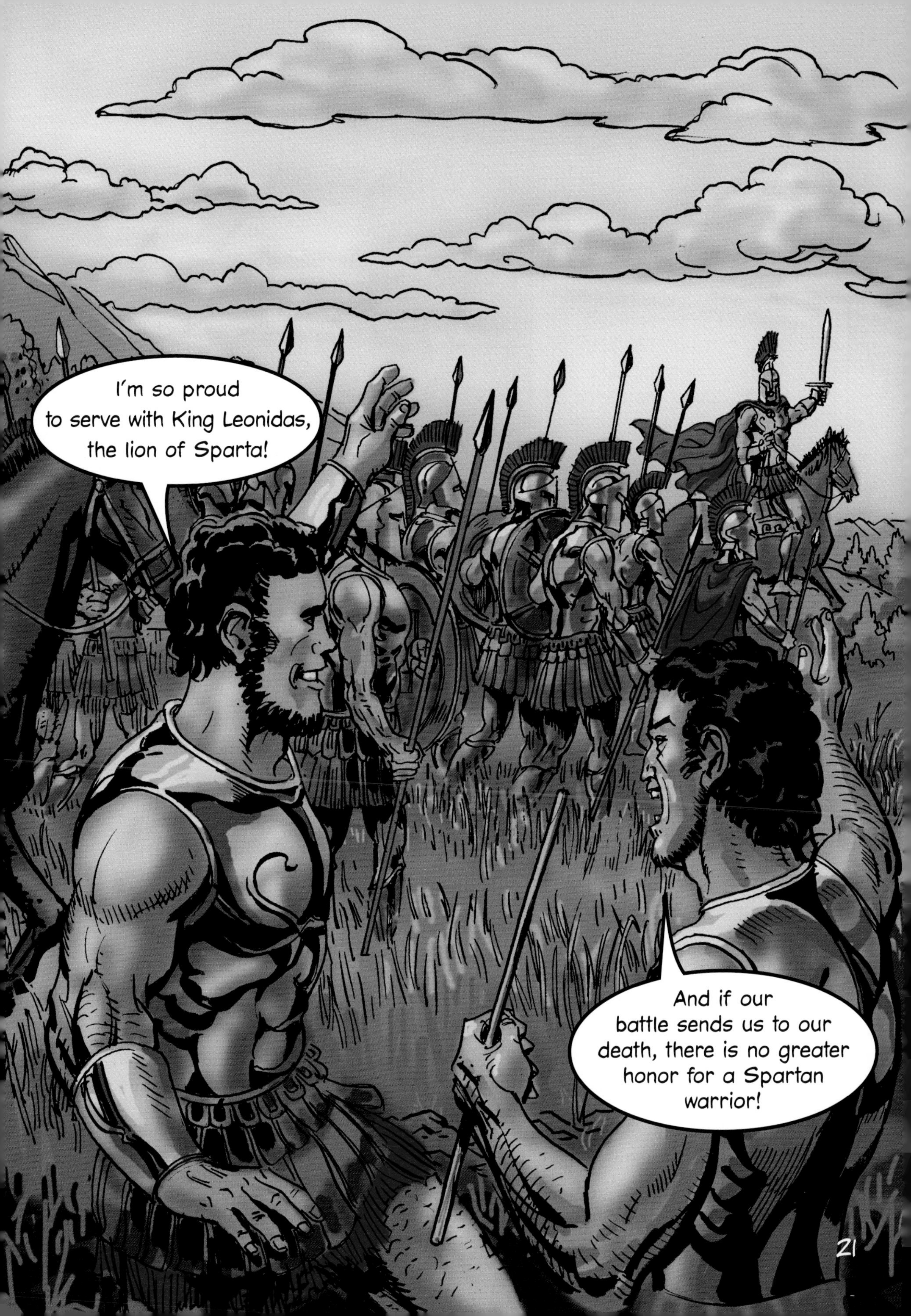
I'm so proud to serve with King Leonidas, the lion of Sparta!
And if our battle sends us to our death, there is no greater honor for a Spartan warrior!

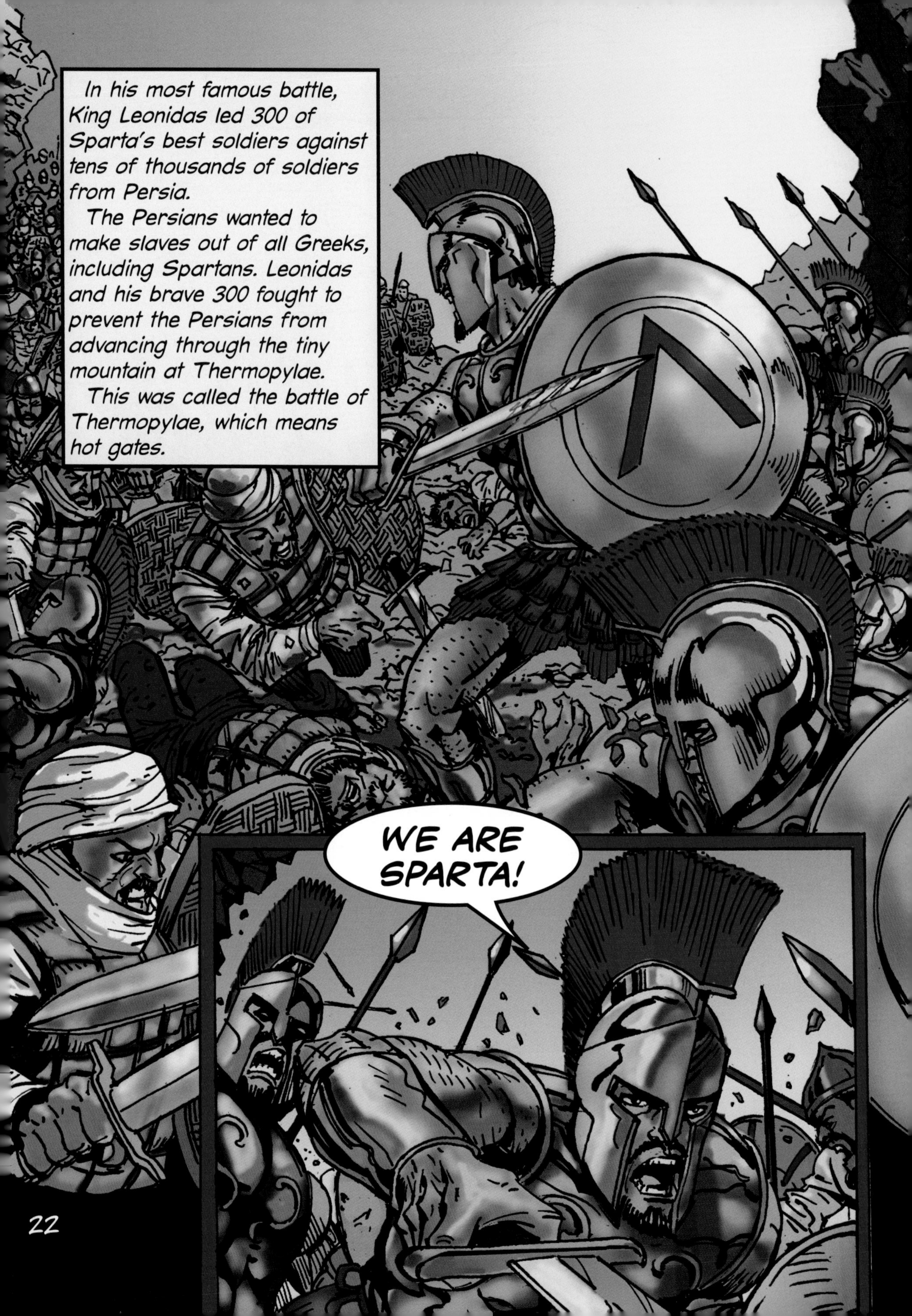
In his most famous battle, King Leonidas led 300 of Sparta's best soldiers against tens of thousands of soldiers from Persia.
The Persians wanted to make slaves out of all Greeks, including Spartans. Leonidas and his brave 300 fought to prevent the Persians from advancing through the tiny mountain at Thermopylae.
This was called the battle of Thermopylae, which means hot gates.
WE ARE SPARTA!

On the first two days of battle, the brave Spartan army killed as many as 70,000 Persian soldiers. Only 20 Spartans died. But the Spartans were outnumbered. King Leonidas was among those who died in the battle, but his death made him a bigger hero than ever before. Because of King Leonidas's brave 300, Persia didn't make slaves of the Spartans.

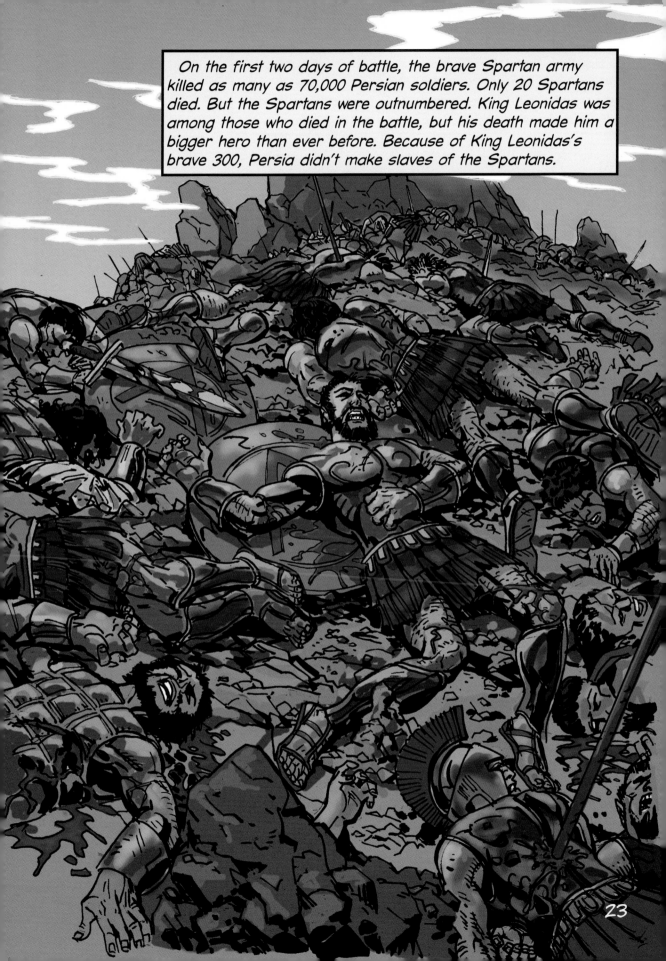

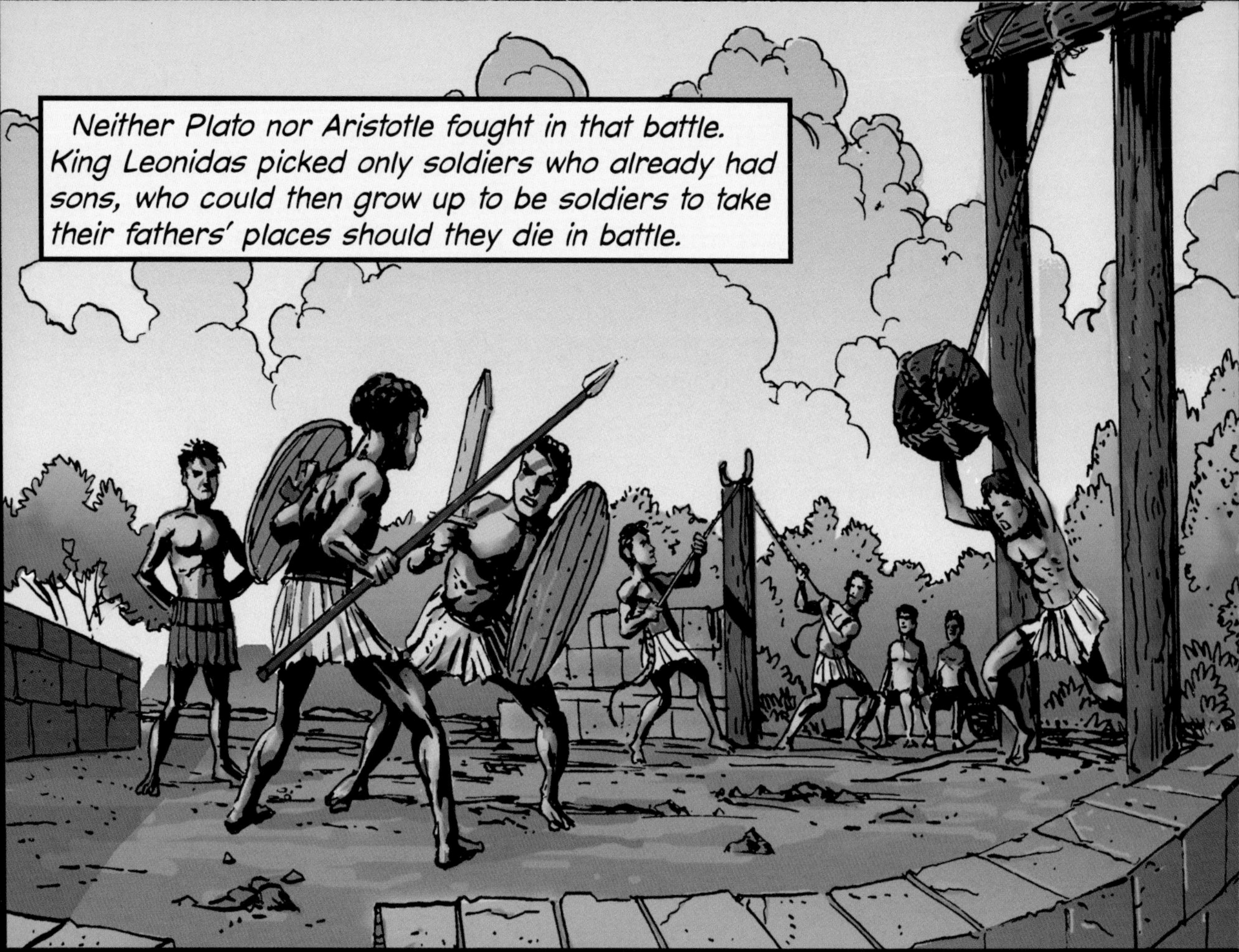
Neither Plato nor Aristotle fought in that battle. King Leonidas picked only soldiers who already had sons, who could then grow up to be soldiers to take their fathers' places should they die in battle.

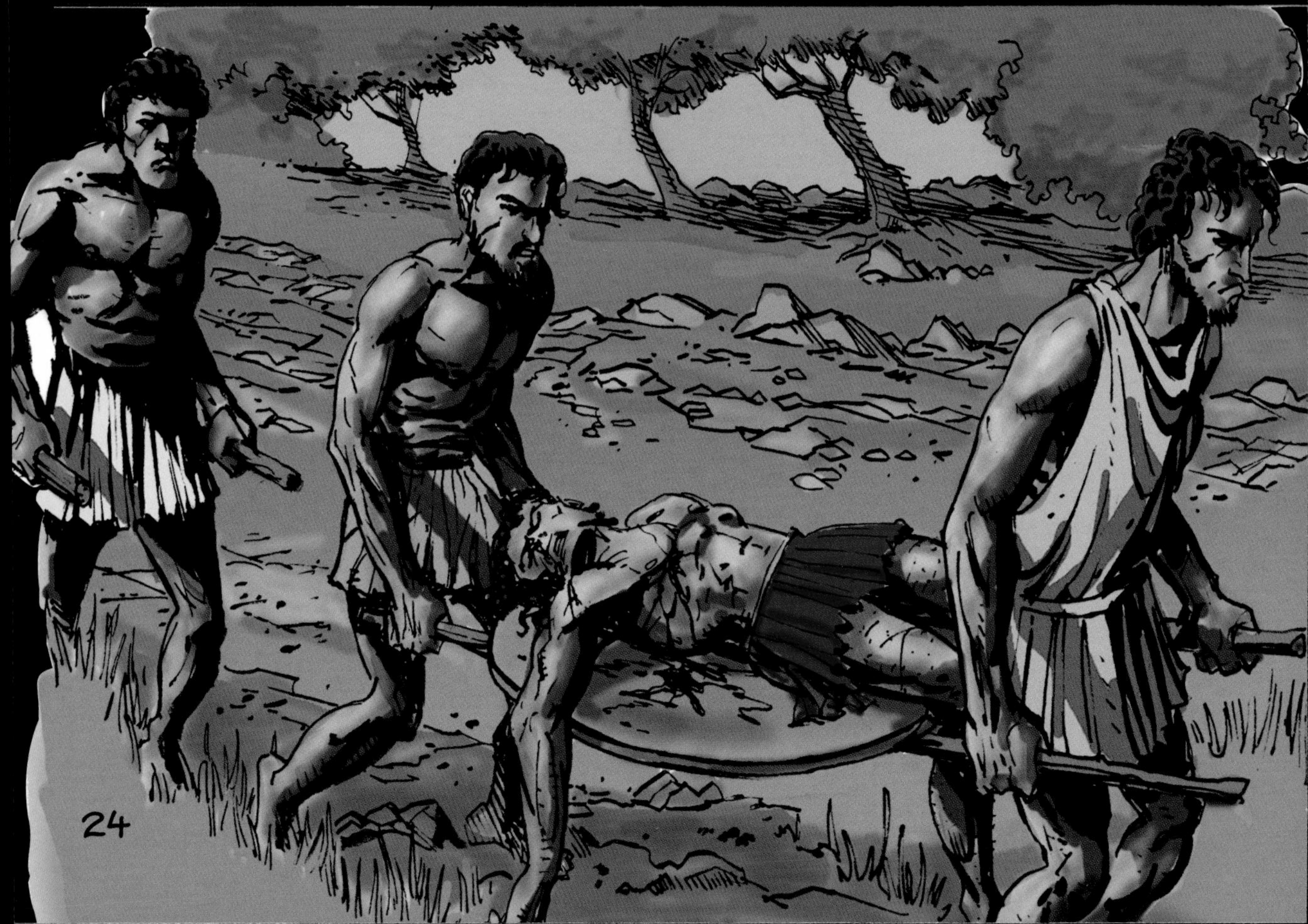

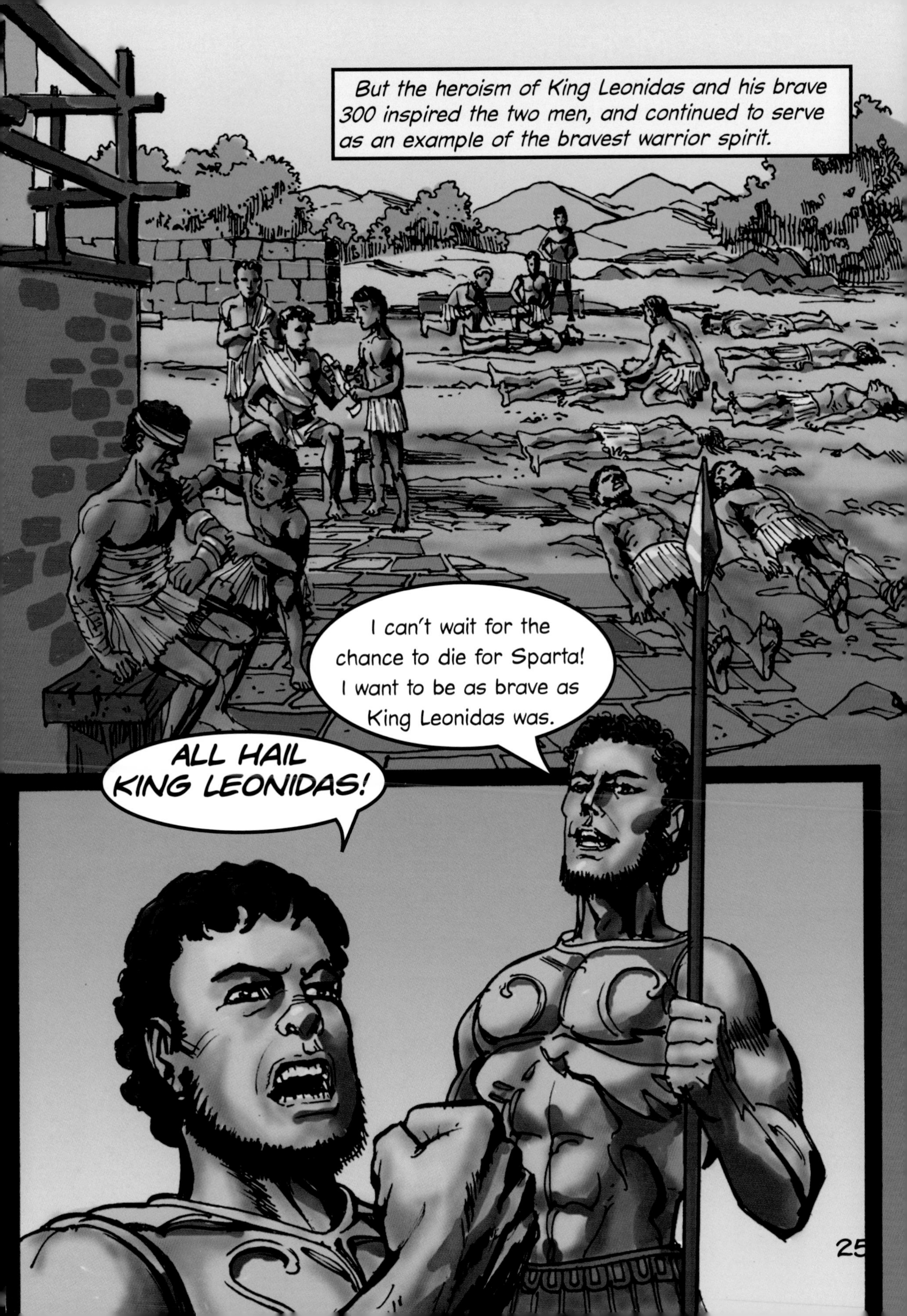

But the heroism of King Leonidas and his brave 300 inspired the two men, and continued to serve as an example of the bravest warrior spirit.
I can't wait for the chance to die for Sparta! I want to be as brave as King Leonidas was.
ALL HAIL KING LEONIDAS!

During the era around 500 B.C., **Sparta** was the strongest and most powerful city-state in ancient Greece. Its people belonged to three classes.

In 936 AD, Sparta was destroyed by the Visigoths. However, in 1834 a New Sparta was built near the location of the original city.

The ruling class was called **Spartans**, and they were free citizens who treated most of the others who lived in Sparta as slaves.

The slaves were called **Helots**. There were ten times as many helots as there were Spartans.

The third and smallest group were Greeks who weren't Spartans, but who were treated as free people rather than slaves. They were called **Perioeci**.

Farming was the main way of life for Spartan families, though helots did most of the work.

Spartan boys were raised to be soldiers. From birth they were said to belong to the state rather than their families, and they spent most of their life from boyhood on in the military.

It wasn't until a Spartan man turned 30 that he became a full citizen, with the right to marry and hold public office.

He didn't retire from the military until he turned 60, and even then he might still train boys to be soldiers.

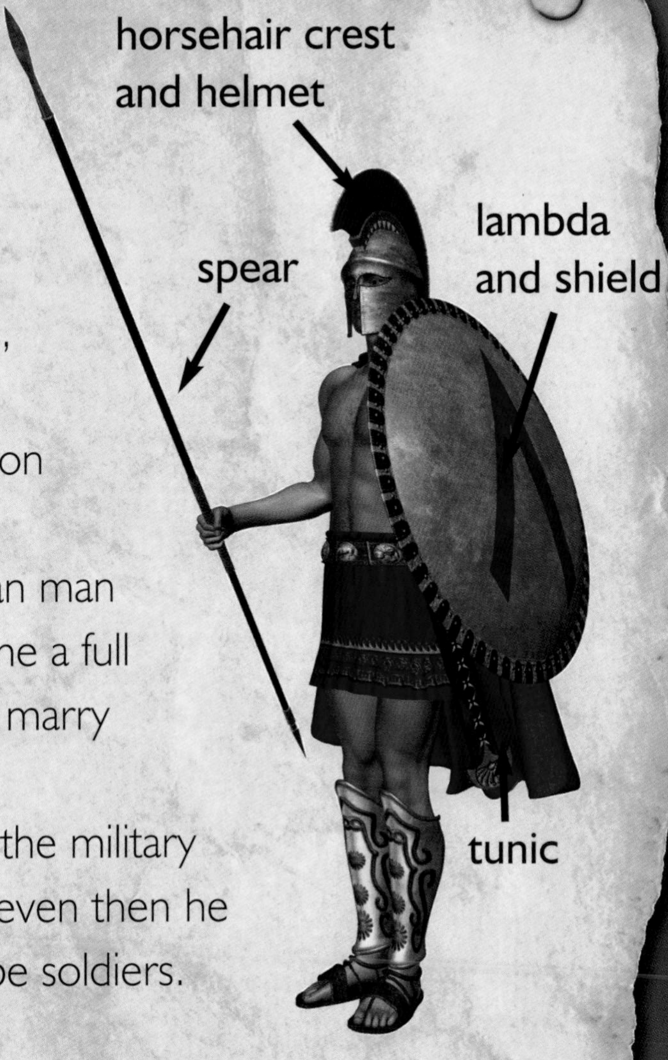
horsehair crest and helmet
lambda and shield
spear
tunic

When a Spartan warrior was injured or died in battle, he was carried home on his shield.

Spartan girls and women had more freedom than any others in Greece. They enjoyed athletic competitions when they were young. When they were older and married to a soldier, they ran their own households, as their husbands were often away at war.

King Leonidas is often remembered in statues.

Even though Sparta was eventually defeated by the Roman Empire, the proud Spartan warrior lives on today mainly in the memory and history.

Timeline

In 480 BC, King Leonidas was killed at the Battle of Thermopylae.

In 404 BC, Sparta defeated **Athens**, its major rival.

In 146 BC, Sparta was defeated by the more powerful **Roman Empire**.

In 936 AD, Sparta was destroyed by the Visigoths.

Websites for Further Reading

www.wsu.edu:8080/~dee/GREECE/SPARTA.HTM

www.sikyon.com/Sparta/sparta_eg.html

www.sikyon.com/sparta/history_eg.html

www.history.net.com/greco-persian-wars-battle-of-thermopylae.htm

Glossary

Athens (A-thenz): This city is Sparta's rival in Greece. It is known more for its art and culture than for its warriors.

Helots (HEEL-uhtz): These are Greek slaves in Sparta.

Leonidas, King (lee AHN ih duhs, KING): He was a famous Spartan ruler and warrior.

Perioeci (PARE-ee-EE-see): These are the non-Spartans who were not slaves.

Persia (PURR-zhuh): The country that is now Iran (and part of Afghanistan). Their warriors fought the Spartans in the Battle of Thermopylae.

Roman Empire (ROH-mun EM-pire): This is a group of countries ruled by Rome, in what is now Italy.

Sparta (SPAR-tuh): This was a city-state in the south of ancient Greece.

Spartans (SPAR-tunz): These were citizens of Sparta.

Thermopylae, Battle of (thuhr MAHP uh lee, BAT-uhl uhv): This was a mountain pass in ancient Greece, with a name that means hot gates. This was the site of the famous battle between the Greeks and the Persians.

Index

Athens   29

farming   26

Helots   26

King Leonidas   5, 20, 21,
    22, 23, 24, 25, 28

military   4, 5, 11, 27

Perioeci   26

Persia   22, 23

Persian(s)   5, 22, 23

Roman Empire   28, 29

soldier(s)   7, 9, 11, 12, 17,
    18, 19, 20, 22, 23, 24,
    27, 28

Sparta   5, 8, 9, 10, 11, 20,
    21, 22, 25, 26, 28, 29

Spartan(s)   5, 8, 20, 21,
    22, 23, 26, 27, 28, 29

warrior(s)   6, 8, 11, 16,
    19, 20, 21, 25

About the Author

Don McLeese is a journalism professor at the University of Iowa. He has written many articles for newspapers and magazines and many books for young students as well.

About the Artist

Chris Marrinan is an artist who has created images for many things, including everything from billboards to video game covers! He got his start in the comic book business drawing for comic book publishers DC Comics, Marvel, Dark Horse, and Image. Chris has drawn many comic icons, such as Wonder Woman, Spider-Man, and Wolverine. He lives in Northern California with his two children.